Journal Edition

FAITH, HOPE & LOVE

Journal Edition

FAITH, HOPE & LOVE

Saint AUGUSTINE

WHITAKER HOUSE

Publisher's Note: This edition has been slightly updated for the modern reader. Some words, spellings, and sentence structure have been revised for clarity and readability.

Faith, Hope, and Love
Journal Edition
(Originally published as *The Enchiridion on Faith, Hope, and Love* or *Handbook of Faith, Hope, and Love.*)

Translated by Albert C. Outler

ISBN: 978-1-62911-928-1
eBook ISBN: 978-1-62911-929-8
Printed in the United States of America

Whitaker House
1030 Hunt Valley Circle
New Kensington, PA 15068
www.whitakerhouse.com

Library of Congress Cataloging-in-Publication Data (Pending)

1 2 3 4 5 6 7 8 9 10 24 23 22 21 20 19 18

Contents

About the Author

Aurelius Augustinus (354–430), better known as Saint Augustine, was born to poor parents in the small town of Tagaste in Numidia, North Africa. His father, Patricius, a pagan who lived somewhat of a loose life, was converted to Christianity before his death; his mother, Monnica, is one of the most revered women in the history of the Christian church on account of her personal piety and influence on her son.

Augustine was educated at the University of Carthage; according to his own account, he belonged to a group of rowdy friends and joined in their intemperate living. While at the university, he entered into a fourteen-year relationship with a young woman who became the mother of his son, Adeodatus. He also joined the heretical sect of the Manicheans, who professed to have received from their founder a higher form of truth than was taught by Christ.

At the close of his university career, which had been brilliant and full of literary accomplishments, despite distractions, Augustine returned to Tagaste. There, and later in Carthage and Rome, he taught rhetoric, training young lawyers in the art of debate. By the age of twenty-seven,

Augustine had begun doubting the validity of the Manichean faith, and soon thereafter he was converted to Christianity. Augustine's conversion, one of the most renowned in church history, occurred after he repeatedly heard a voice say, "Take up and read." Alone in a garden, Augustine interpreted the voice as a command from God, and he instantly picked up the Scriptures. The first passage he came across, Romans 13:13–14, profoundly affected him, and he acknowledged Christ as the only way to salvation. Augustine was baptized the following year, gave up his teaching profession, and became an ascetic—studying the foundations of faith, writing (chiefly against his former sect), and conversing with a group of disciples, first in Rome and then in his native town.

During a visit to Hippo, a town not far from Tagaste, Augustine was encouraged to enter the priesthood and did so. In 395, he became Bishop of Hippo, an office he filled for the remaining thirty-five years of his life. Though he took a leading part in the activities of the African church and gradually became one of the most distinguished ecclesiastical figures in the Roman Empire, the care of his diocese and the writing of books formed his chief occupations. He continued to lead a life of extreme simplicity and self-denial and, in his pastoral establishment, trained a large number of disciples who became leaders in the church. Augustine's influence on these younger men was due not only to his intellectual ascendancy but also to the tenderness of his disposition.

A bulk of Augustine's literary activity was devoted to refuting heresies of his time. His two most important books are *The City of God*—which compares the "City of Man," founded upon self-love, with the "City of God," founded upon self-denial and love for God—and *The Confessions*. The latter work remains unsurpassed as a sincere and intimate record of a great and pious soul laid bare before God.

About the Work

"I also wrote a book on Faith, Hope, and Charity, on the request of the person to whom I addressed it, that he might have a work of mine which should never be out of his hands, such as the Greeks call an Enchiridion. There I think I have pretty carefully treated of the manner in which God is to be worshipped, which knowledge divine Scripture defines to be the true wisdom of man."

—St. Augustine,
from his book *Retractations, I. ii. c. 63*

When he was about sixty-six years old, Augustine of Hippo broke from writing *The City of God* to pen this enchiridion, or handbook. It is addressed to Laurentius, in answer to questions the man had posed to the author. Although specifics about this person are otherwise unknown, one manuscript refers to him as a deacon, another as a notary of the city of Rome. He was most likely an important layman in the church. St. Augustine wrote the work sometime after the death of Jerome (September 30, 420), for he alludes in section 87 to "the presbyter Jerome, of holy memory."

This small volume is arguably the most practical and down-to-earth of Augustine's writings. Indeed, it was intended as a handbook, literally, to be carried in the hand and not stuffed away in some library. In it, Augustine subdivides the chief purpose of the Christian life into the three virtues listed in 1 Corinthians 13:13—faith, hope, and love. For faith, Augustine examines the Apostles' Creed. For hope, he gives a brief exposition of the Lord's Prayer. He finishes with a discourse on Christian love. Augustine displays an optimistic tone, firmly based upon the inevitable demise of evil and the triumph of goodness. Throughout, Augustine does not write as an ivory-towered theologian, nor as an ethereal mystic, but as a grounded monk who is not immune to sin—a redeemed man who is grateful, earnestly repentant, and utterly dependent upon the pervasive mercies of God.

In a modern world so full of skepticism, despondency, and corruption, this word of encouragement from an important early church father to an earnest seeker of truth continues to provide us with enduring enlightenment regarding the kingdom of God and the ultimate triumph of good over evil.

—*Whitaker House*

1

The Occasion and Purpose of this "Manual"

1. I cannot express, my dearest son Laurentius, how much your learning pleases me, and how much I desire that you should be wise—though not one of those of whom it is said: *"Where is the wise? where is the scribe? where is the disputer of this world? hath not God made foolish the wisdom of this world?"*[1] Rather, you should be one of those of whom it is written, "The multitude of the wise is the welfare of the world"[2]; and also you should be the kind of man the apostle wishes those men to be to whom he said, *"I would have you wise unto that which is good, and simple concerning evil."*[3]

2. Human wisdom consists in piety. This you have in the book of the saintly Job, for there he writes that wisdom herself said to man, *"Behold,* [piety], *that is wisdom."*[4] If, then, you ask what kind of piety she was speaking of, you will find it more distinctly designated by the Greek term *theosebeia,* literally, "the service of God." The Greek has

1. 1 Corinthians 1:20.
2. Wisdom of Solomon 6:24 (Apocrypha).
3. Romans 16:19. A later interpolation, not found in the best manuscripts, adds, "As no one can exist from himself, so also no one can be wise in himself save only as he is enlightened by Him of whom it is written, 'All wisdom is from God' (Ecclesiasticus 1:1)."
4. Job 28:28.

still another word for "piety," *ensebeia,* which also signifies "proper service." This too refers chiefly to the service of God. But no term is better than *theosebeia,* which clearly expresses the idea of the man's service of God as the source of human wisdom.

When you ask me to be brief, you do not expect me to speak of great issues in a few sentences, do you? Is not this rather what you desire: a brief summary or a short treatise on the proper mode of worshipping (serving) God?

3. If I should answer, "God should be worshipped in faith, hope, love," you would doubtless reply that this was shorter than you wished, and might then beg for a brief explication of what each of these three means: What should be believed, what should be hoped for, and what should be loved? If I should answer these questions, you would then have everything you asked for in your letter. If you have kept a copy of it, you can easily refer to it. If not, recall your questions as I discuss them.

4. It is your desire, as you wrote, to have from me a book, a sort of enchiridion,[5] as it might be called—something to have "at hand"—that deals with your questions. What is to be sought after above all else? What, in view of the divers heresies, is to be avoided above all else? How far does reason support religion; or what happens to reason when the issues involved

---

5. A transliteration of the Greek *encheiridion,* literally, a handbook or manual.

concern faith alone; what is the beginning and end of our endeavor? What is the most comprehensive of all explanations? What is the certain and distinctive foundation of the Catholic faith? You would have the answers to all these questions if you really understood what a man should believe, what he should hope for, and what he ought to love. For these are the chief things—indeed, the only things—to seek for in religion. He who turns away from them is either a complete stranger to the name of Christ or else he is a heretic. Things that arise in sensory experience, or that are analyzed by the intellect, may be demonstrated by the reason. But in matters that pass beyond the scope of the physical senses, which we have not settled by our own understanding, and cannot—here we must believe, without hesitation, the witness of those men by whom the Scriptures (rightly called divine) were composed, men who were divinely aided in their senses and their minds to see and even to foresee the things about which they testify.

5. But, as this faith, which works by love,[6] begins to penetrate the soul, it tends, through the vital power of goodness, to change into sight, so that the holy and perfect in heart catch glimpses of that ineffable beauty whose full vision is our highest happiness. Here, then, surely, is the answer to your question about the beginning and the end of our endeavor. We begin in faith, we are perfected

6. See Galatians 5:6.

in sight.[7] This likewise is the most comprehensive of all explanations. As for the certain and distinctive foundation of the Catholic faith, it is Christ. *"For other foundation,"* said the apostle, *"can no man lay than that is laid, which is Christ Jesus."*[8] Nor should it be denied that this is the distinctive basis of the Catholic faith, just because it appears that it is common to us and to certain heretics as well. For if we think carefully about the meaning of Christ, we shall see that among some of the heretics who wish to be called Christians, the name of Christ is held in honor, but the reality itself is not among them. To make all this plain would take too long—because we would then have to review all the heresies that have been, the ones that now exist, and those which could exist under the label "Christian," and we would have to show that what we have said of all is true of each of them. Such a discussion would take so many volumes as to make it seem endless.[9]

6. You have asked for an enchiridion, something you could carry around, not just baggage for your bookshelf. Therefore we may return to these three ways in which, as we said, God should be served: faith, hope, and love. It is easy to say what one ought to believe, what to hope for, and what to love. But to defend our doctrines against the

7. See 1 Corinthians 13:10–11.
8. 1 Corinthians 3:11.
9. Already, very early in his ministry (397), Augustine had written *De Agone Christiano,* in which he had reviewed and refuted a full score of heresies threatening the orthodox faith.

calumnies of those who think differently is a more difficult and detailed task. If one is to have this wisdom, it is not enough just to put an enchiridion in the hand. It is also necessary that a great zeal be kindled in the heart.

2

The Creed and the Lord's Prayer as Guides to the Interpretation of the Theological Virtues of Faith, Hope, and Love

7. Let us begin, for example, with the symbol[10] and the Lord's Prayer. What is shorter to hear or to read? What is more easily memorized? Since through sin the human race stood grievously burdened by great misery and in deep need of mercy, a prophet, preaching of the time of God's grace, said, *"And it shall come to pass, that whosoever shall call on the name of the LORD shall be delivered."*[11] Thus, we have the Lord's Prayer.

Later, the apostle, when he wished to commend this same grace, remembered this prophetic testimony and promptly added, *"How then shall they call on him in whom they have not believed?"*[12] Thus, we have the symbol. In these two we have the three theological virtues working together: faith believes; hope and love pray. Yet without faith nothing else is possible; thus faith prays too. This, then, is the meaning of the saying, *"How shall they call on him in whom they have not believed?"*

10. The Apostles' Creed. See Augustine's early essay *On Faith and the Creed.*
11. Joel 2:32.
12. Romans 10:14.

8. Now, is it possible to hope for what we do not believe in? We can, of course, believe in something that we do not hope for. Who among the faithful does not believe in the punishment of the impious? Yet he does not hope for it, and whoever believes that such a punishment is threatening him and draws back in horror from it is more rightly said to fear than to hope. A poet, distinguishing between these two feelings, said, "Let those who dread be allowed to hope,"[13] but another poet, and a better one, did not put it rightly: "Here, if I could have hoped for [i.e., foreseen] such a grievous blow."[14]

Indeed, some grammarians use this as an example of inaccurate language and comment, "He said 'to hope' when he should have said 'to fear.'" Therefore faith may refer to evil things as well as to good, since we believe in both the good and evil. Yet faith is good, not evil. Moreover, faith refers to things past and present and future. For we believe that Christ died; this is a past event. We believe that He sits at the Father's right hand; this is present. We believe that He will come as our judge; this is future. Again, faith has to do with our own affairs and with those of others. For everyone believes, both about himself and other persons—and about things as well—that at some time He began to exist and that He has not existed forever. Thus,

13. Lucan, *Pharsalia*, 2, 15.

14. Virgil, *Aeneid*, 4, 419. The context of this quotation is Dido's lament over Aeneas' prospective abandonment of her. She is saying that if she could have foreseen such a disaster, she would have been able to bear it. Augustine's criticism here is a literalistic quibble.

not only about men, but even about angels, we believe many things that have a bearing on religion.

But hope deals only with good things, and only with those that lie in the future, and that pertain to the man who cherishes the hope. Since this is so, faith must be distinguished from hope: they are different terms and likewise different concepts. Yet faith and hope have this in common: they refer to what is not seen, whether this unseen is believed in or hoped for. Thus in the epistle to the Hebrews, which is used by the enlightened defenders of the catholic rule of faith, faith is said to be *"the evidence of things not seen."*[15] However, when a man maintains that neither words nor witnesses nor even arguments, but only the evidence of present experience, determine his faith, he still ought not to be called absurd or told, "You have seen; therefore you have not believed." For it does not follow that unless a thing is not seen it cannot be believed. Still it is better for us to use the term "faith," as we are taught in "the sacred eloquence,"[16] to refer to things not seen. And as for hope, the apostle says: *"Hope that is seen is not hope: for what a man seeth, why doth he yet hope for? But if we hope for that we see not, then do we with patience wait for it."*[17] When, therefore, our good is believed to be future, this is the same thing as hoping for it.

15. Hebrews 11:1.

16. *Sacra eloquia*—a favorite phrase of Augustine's for the Bible.

17. Romans 8:24–25.

What, then, shall I say of love, without which faith can do nothing? There can be no true hope without love. Indeed, as the apostle James says, *"The devils also believe, and tremble."*[18]

Yet they neither hope nor love. Instead, believing as we do that what we hope for and love is coming to pass, they tremble. Therefore, the apostle Paul approves and commends the faith that works by love and that cannot exist without hope. Thus it is that love is not without hope, hope is not without love, and neither hope nor love are without faith.

18. James 2:19.

3

God the Creator of All; and the Goodness of All Creation

9. Wherefore, when it is asked what we ought to believe in matters of religion, the answer is not to be sought in the exploration of the nature of things (*rerum natura*), after the manner of those whom the Greeks called "physicists."[19] Nor should we be dismayed if Christians are ignorant about the properties and the number of the basic elements of nature, or about the motion, order, and deviations of the stars, the map of the heavens, the kinds and nature of animals, plants, stones, springs, rivers, and mountains; about the divisions of space and time, about the signs of impending storms, and the myriad other things which these "physicists" have come to understand, or think they have. For even these men, gifted with such superior insight, with their ardor in study and their abundant leisure, exploring some of these matters by human conjecture and others through historical inquiry, have not yet learned everything there is to know. For that matter,

19. One of the standard titles of early Greek philosophical treatises was: *pi epsilon rho iota phi nu sigma epsilon omega zeta,* which would translate into Latin as *De rerum natura*. This is, in fact, the title of Lucretius' famous poem, the greatest philosophical work written in classical Latin.

many of the things they are so proud to have discovered are more often matters of opinion than of verified knowledge.

For the Christian, it is enough to believe that the cause of all created things, whether in heaven or on earth, whether visible or invisible, is nothing other than the goodness of the Creator, who is the one and the true God.[20] Further, the Christian believes that nothing exists save God Himself and what comes from Him; and he believes that God is triune, i.e., the Father, and the Son begotten of the Father, and the Holy Spirit proceeding from the same Father, but one and the same Spirit of the Father and the Son.

10. By this Trinity, supremely and equally and immutably good, were all things created. But they were not created supremely, equally, nor immutably good. Still, each single created thing is good, and taken as a whole they are very good, because together they constitute a universe of admirable beauty.

11. In this universe, even what is called evil, when it is rightly ordered and kept in its place, commends the good more eminently, since good things yield greater pleasure and praise when compared to the bad things. For the Omnipotent God, whom even the heathen acknowledge as the Supreme Power over all, would not allow any evil in His works, unless in His omnipotence and goodness, as the Supreme Good, He is able to bring forth good out

20. This basic motif appears everywhere in Augustine's thought as the very foundation of his whole system.

of evil. What, after all, is anything we call evil except the privation of good? In animal bodies, for instance, sickness and wounds are nothing but the privation of health. When a cure is effected, the evils that were present (i.e., the sickness and the wounds) do not retreat and go elsewhere. Rather, they simply do not exist anymore. For such evil is not a substance; the wound or the disease is a defect of the bodily substance which, as a substance, is good. Evil, then, is an accident, i.e., a privation of that good which is called health. Thus, whatever defects there are in a soul are privations of a natural good. When a cure takes place, they are not transferred elsewhere but, since they are no longer present in the state of health, they no longer exist at all.[21]

21. This section (chapters 3 and 4) is the most explicit statement of a major motif which pervades the whole of Augustinian metaphysics. We see it in his earliest writings, *Soliloquies*, 1, 2, and *De Ordine*, 2:7. It is obviously a part of the Neoplatonic heritage that Augustine appropriated for his Christian philosophy. The good is positive, constructive, essential; evil is privative, destructive, parasitic on the good. It has its origin, not in nature, but in the will. See *Confessions*, Book 7, Chapters 3, 5, 12–16; *On Continence*, 14–16; *Tractates on the Gospel of John*, 98:7; *City of God*, 11:17; 12:7–9.

4

The Problem of Evil

12. All of nature, therefore, is good, since the Creator of all nature is supremely good. But nature is not supremely and immutably good as is the Creator of it. Thus the good in created things can be diminished and augmented. For good to be diminished is evil; still, however much it is diminished, something must remain of its original nature as long as it exists at all. For no matter what kind or however insignificant a thing may be, the good that is its "nature" cannot be destroyed without the thing itself being destroyed. There is good reason, therefore, to praise an uncorrupted thing, and if it were indeed an incorruptible thing which could not be destroyed, it would doubtless be all the more worthy of praise. When, however, a thing is corrupted, its corruption is an evil because it is, by just so much, a privation of the good. Where there is no privation of the good, there is no evil.

Where there is evil, there is a corresponding diminution of the good. As long, then, as a thing is being corrupted, there is good in it of which it is being deprived; and in this process, if something of its being remains that cannot be further corrupted, this will then be an incorruptible entity (*natura incorruptibilis*), and to this great good it will have come through the process of corruption.

But even if the corruption is not arrested, it still does not cease having some good of which it cannot be further deprived. If, however, the corruption comes to be total and entire, there is no good left either, because it is no longer an entity at all. Wherefore corruption cannot consume the good without also consuming the thing itself. Every actual entity (*natura*) is therefore good; a greater good if it cannot be corrupted, a lesser good if it can be. Yet only the foolish and unknowing can deny that it is still good even when corrupted. Whenever a thing is consumed by corruption, not even the corruption remains, for it is nothing in itself, having no subsistent being in which to exist.

13. From this it follows that there is nothing to be called evil if there is nothing good. A good that wholly lacks an evil aspect is entirely good. Where there is some evil in a thing, its good is defective or defectible. Thus there can be no evil where there is no good. This leads us to a surprising conclusion: that, since every being, in so far as it is a being, is good, if we then say that a defective thing is bad, it would seem to mean that we are saying that what is evil is good, that only what is good is ever evil and that there is no evil apart from something good. This is because every actual entity is good (*omnis natura bonum est*). Nothing evil exists in itself, but only as an evil aspect of some actual entity. Therefore, there can be nothing evil except something good. Absurd as this sounds, nevertheless the logical connections of the argument compel us to it as inevitable. At the same time, we must take warning lest we incur the

prophetic judgment which reads: "*Woe unto them that call evil good, and good evil; that put darkness for light, and light for darkness; that put bitter for sweet, and sweet for bitter!*"[22] Moreover the Lord Himself said: "*An evil man out of the evil treasure bringeth forth evil things.*"[23] What, then, is an evil man but an evil entity (*natura mala*), since man is an entity? Now, if a man is something good because he is an entity, what, then, is a bad man except an evil good? When, however, we distinguish between these two concepts, we find that the bad man is not bad because he is a man, nor is he good because he is wicked. Rather, he is a good entity in so far as he is a man, evil in so far as he is wicked. Therefore, if anyone says that simply to be a man is evil, or that to be a wicked man is good, he rightly falls under the prophetic judgment: "*Woe unto them who call evil good, and good evil.*"

For this amounts to finding fault with God's work, because man is an entity of God's creation. It also means that we are praising the defects in this particular man because he is a wicked person. Thus, every entity, even if it is a defective one, in so far as it is an entity, is good. In so far as it is defective, it is evil.

14. Actually, then, in these two contraries we call evil and good, the rule of the logicians fails to apply.[24] No weather is both dark and bright at the same time; no food or drink is both sweet and sour at the same time; nobody is, at the same time and place, both white and black, nor

22. Isaiah 5:20.

23. Matthew 12:35.

24. This refers to Aristotle's well-known principle of "the excluded middle."

deformed and well-formed at the same time. This principle is found to apply in almost all disjunctions: two contraries cannot coexist in a single thing. Nevertheless, while no one maintains that good and evil are not contraries, they can not only coexist, but the evil cannot exist at all without the good, or in a thing that is not a good. On the other hand, the good can exist without evil. For a man or an angel could exist and yet not be wicked, whereas there cannot be wickedness except in a man or an angel. It is good to be a man, good to be an angel; but evil to be wicked. These two contraries are thus coexistent, so that if there were no good in what is evil, then the evil simply could not be, since it can have no mode in which to exist, nor any source from which corruption springs, unless it be something corruptible. Unless this something is good, it cannot be corrupted, because corruption is nothing more than the deprivation of the good.

Evils, therefore, have their source in the good, and unless they are parasitic on something good, they are not anything at all. There is no other source whence an evil thing can come to be. If this is the case, then, in so far as a thing is an entity, it is unquestionably good. If it is an incorruptible entity, it is a great good. But even if it is a corruptible entity, it still has no mode of existence except as an aspect of something that is good. Only by corrupting something good can corruption inflict injury.

15. But when we say that evil has its source in the good, do not suppose that this denies our Lord's

judgment: *"A good tree cannot bring forth evil fruit."*[25] This cannot be, even as the Truth Himself declares: *"For of thorns men do not gather figs,"*[26] since thorns cannot bear grapes. Nevertheless, from good soil we can see both vines and thorns spring up. Likewise, just as a bad tree does not grow good fruit, so also an evil will does not produce good deeds. From a human nature, which is good in itself, there can spring forth either a good or an evil will. There was no other place from whence evil could have arisen in the first place except from the nature—good in itself—of an angel or a man. This is what our Lord Himself most clearly shows in the passage about the trees and the fruits, for He said: *"Make the tree good, and his fruit good; or else make the tree corrupt, and his fruit corrupt."*[27] This is warning enough that bad fruit cannot grow on a good tree nor good fruit on a bad one. Yet from that same earth to which He was referring, both sorts of trees can grow.

25. Matthew 7:18.
26. Luke 6:44.
27. Matthew 12:33.

5

The Kinds and Degrees of Error

16. This being the case, when that verse of Maro's gives us pleasure, "Happy is he who can understand the causes of things,"[28] it still does not follow that our felicity depends upon our knowing the causes of the great physical processes in the world, which are hidden in the secret maze of nature, "Whence earthquakes, whose force swells the sea to flood, so that they burst their bounds and then subside again,"[29] and other such things as this.

But we ought to know the causes of good and evil in things, at least as far as men may do so in this life, filled as it is with errors and distress, in order to avoid these errors and distresses. We must always aim at that true felicity wherein misery does not distract, nor error mislead. If it is a good thing to understand the causes of physical motion, there is nothing of greater concern in these matters that we ought to understand than our own health. But when we are in ignorance of such things, we seek out a physician, who has seen how the secrets of heaven and earth still remain hidden from us, and what patience there must be in unknowing.

---

28. Virgil, *Georgios,* 2:490.
29. Ibid., 479.

17. Although we should beware of error wherever possible, not only in great matters but in small ones as well, it is impossible not to be ignorant of many things. Yet it does not follow that one falls into error out of ignorance alone. If someone thinks he knows what he does not know, if he approves as true what is actually false, this then is error, in the proper sense of the term. Obviously, much depends on the question involved in the error, for in one and the same question one naturally prefers the instructed to the ignorant, the expert to the blunderer, and this with good reason. In a complex issue, however, as when one man knows one thing and another man knows something else, if the former knowledge is more useful and the latter is less useful or even harmful, who in this latter case would not prefer ignorance? There are some things, after all, that it is better not to know than to know.

Likewise, there is sometimes profit in error—but on a journey, not in morals.[30] This sort of thing happened to us once, when we mistook the way at a crossroads and did not go by the place where an armed gang of Donatists lay in wait to ambush us. We finally arrived at the place where we were going, but only by a roundabout way, and upon learning of the ambush, we were glad to have erred and gave thanks to God for our error. Who would doubt, in such a situation, that the erring traveler is better off than the unerring brigand? This perhaps explains the meaning of our finest poet, when he speaks for an unhappy lover:

30. *Sed in via pedum, non in via morum.*

"When I saw [her] I was undone, and fatal error swept me away,"[31] for there is such a thing as a fortunate mistake which not only does no harm but actually does some good.

But now for a more careful consideration of the truth in this business: to *err* means nothing more than to judge as true what is in fact false, and as false what is true. It means to be certain about the uncertain, uncertain about the certain, whether it be certainly true or certainly false. This sort of error in the mind is deforming and improper, since the fitting and proper thing would be to be able to say, in speech or judgment: "Yes, yes. No, no."[32] Actually, the wretched lives we lead come partly from this: that sometimes if they are not to be entirely lost, error is unavoidable. It is different in that higher life where truth itself is the life of our souls, where none deceives and none is deceived. In this life men deceive and are deceived, and are actually worse off when they deceive by lying than when they are deceived by believing lies. Yet our rational mind shrinks from falsehood, and naturally avoids error as much as it can, so that even a deceiver is unwilling to be deceived by somebody else.[33] For the liar thinks he does not deceive himself and that he deceives only those who believe him. Indeed, he does not err in his lying, if he himself knows what the truth is. But he is deceived in

31. Virgil, *Eclogue*, 8:42. The context of the passage is Damon's complaint over his faithless Nyssa; he is here remembering the first time he ever saw her—when he was twelve! See *Theocritus*, 2:82.
32. See Matthew 5:37.
33. See *Confessions*, Book 10, Chapter 23.

this, that he supposes that his lie does no harm to himself, when actually every sin harms the one who commits it more than it does the one who suffers it.

6

The Problem of Lying

18. Here a most difficult and complex issue arises that I once dealt with in a large book, in response to the urgent question whether it is ever the duty of a righteous man to lie.[34] Some go so far as to contend that in cases concerning the worship of God or even the nature of God, it is sometimes a good and pious deed to speak falsely. It seems to me, however, that every lie is a sin, albeit there is a great difference depending on the intention and the topic of the lie. He does not sin as much who lies in the attempt to be helpful as the man who lies as a part of a deliberate wickedness. Nor does one who, by lying, sets a traveler on the wrong road do as much harm as one who, by a deceitful lie, perverts the way of a life. Obviously, no one should be adjudged a liar who speaks falsely what he sincerely supposes is the truth, since in his case he does not deceive but rather is deceived.

---

34. *Ad consentium contra mendacium*, CSEL (J. Zycha, ed.), Vol. 41, pp. 469–528; also *Migne*, PL, 40, c. 517-548; English translation by H.B. Jaffee in Deferrari, St. Augustine: *Treatises on Various Subjects* (The Fathers of the Church, New York, 1952), pp. 113-179. This had been written about a year earlier than *The Enchiridion*. Augustine had also written another treatise *On Lying* much earlier, c. 395; see *De Mendacio* in CSEL (J. Zycha, ed.), Vol. 41, pp. 413–466; *Migne*, PL, 40, c. 487–518; English translation by M.S. Muldowney in Deferrari, op. cit., pp. 47-109. This summary of his position here represents no change of view whatever on this question.

Likewise, a man is not a liar, though he could be charged with rashness, when he incautiously accepts as true what is false. On the other hand, however, that man is a liar in his own conscience who speaks the truth supposing that it is a falsehood. For as far as his soul is concerned, since he did not say what he believed, he did not tell the truth, even though the truth did come out in what he said. Nor is a man to be cleared of the charge of lying whose mouth unknowingly speaks the truth while his conscious intention is to lie. If we do not consider the things spoken of, but only the intentions of the one speaking, he is the better man who unknowingly speaks falsely—because he judges his statement to be true—than the one who unknowingly speaks the truth while in his heart he is attempting to deceive. For the first man does not have one intention in his heart and another in his word, whereas the other, whatever be the facts in his statement, still "has one thought locked in his heart, another ready on his tongue,"[35] which is the very essence of lying. But when we do consider the things spoken of, it makes a great difference in what respect one is deceived or lies. To be deceived is a lesser evil than to lie, as far as a man's intentions are concerned. But it is far more tolerable that a man should lie about things not connected with religion than for one to be deceived in matters where faith and knowledge are prerequisite to the proper service of God. To illustrate what I mean by examples: If one man lies by

35. Sallust, *The War with Catiline*, 10:6–7.

saying that a dead man is alive, and another man, being deceived, believes that Christ will die again after some extended future period—would it not be incomparably better to lie in the first case than to be deceived in the second? And would it not be a lesser evil to lead someone into the former error than to be led by someone into the latter?

19. In some things, then, we are deceived in great matters; in others, small. In some of them no harm is done; in others, even good results. It is a great evil for a man to be deceived so as not to believe what would lead him to life eternal, or what would lead to eternal death. But it is a small evil to be deceived by crediting a falsehood as the truth in a matter where one brings on himself some temporal setback which can then be turned to good use by being borne in faithful patience—as for example, when someone judges a man to be good who is actually bad, and consequently has to suffer evil on his account. Or, take the man who believes a bad man to be good, yet suffers no harm at his hand. He is not badly deceived nor would the prophetic condemnation fall on him: "*Woe unto them who call evil good.*" For we should understand that this saying refers to the things in which men are evil and not to the men themselves. Hence, he who calls adultery a good thing may be rightly accused by the prophetic word. But if he calls a man good supposing him to be chaste and not knowing that he is an adulterer, such a man is not deceived in his doctrine of good and evil, but only as

to the secrets of human conduct. He calls the man good on the basis of what he supposed him to be, and this is undoubtedly a good thing. Moreover, he calls adultery bad and chastity good. But he calls this particular man good in ignorance of the fact that he is an adulterer and not chaste.

In similar fashion, if one escapes an injury through an error, as I mentioned before happened to me on that journey, there is even something good that accrues to a man through his mistakes. But when I say that in such a case a man may be deceived without suffering harm therefrom, or even may gain some benefit thereby, I am not saying that error is not a bad thing, nor that it is a positively good thing. I speak only of the evil that did not happen or the good that did happen, through the error, which was not caused by the error itself but that came out of it. Error, in itself and by itself, whether a great error in great matters or a small error in small affairs, is always a bad thing. For who, except in error, denies that it is bad to approve the false as though it were the truth, or to disapprove the truth as though it were falsehood, or to hold what is certain as if it were uncertain, or what is uncertain as if it were certain? It is one thing to judge a man good who is actually bad—this is an error. It is quite another thing not to suffer harm from something evil if the wicked man whom we supposed to be good actually does nothing harmful to us. It is one thing to suppose that this particular road is the right one when it is not. It is quite another thing that, from this error—which is a bad thing—something good actually turns out, such as being saved from the onslaught of wicked men.

7

Disputed Questions about the Limits of Knowledge and Certainty in Various Matters

20. I do not rightly know whether errors of this sort should be called sins—when one thinks well of a wicked man, not knowing what his character really is, or when, instead of our physical perception, similar perceptions occur which we experience in the spirit (such as the illusion of the apostle Peter when he thought he was seeing a vision but was actually being liberated from fetters and chains by the angel[36]) or in perceptual illusions when we think something is smooth that is actually rough, or something sweet that is bitter, something fragrant that is putrid, that a noise is thunder when it is actually a wagon passing by, when one takes this man for that, or when two men look alike, as happens in the case of twins—whence our poet speaks of "a pleasant error for parents"[37]—say I do not know whether these and other such errors should be called sins.

Nor am I at the moment trying to deal with that knottiest of questions that baffled the most acute men of the academy, whether a wise man ought ever to affirm

36. See Acts 12:9.
37. Virgil, *Aeneid*, 10:392.

anything positively lest he be involved in the error of affirming as true what may be false, since all questions, as they assert, are either mysterious (*occulta*) or uncertain. On these points I wrote three books in the early stages of my conversion because my further progress was being blocked by objections like this, which stood at the very threshold of my understanding.[38] It was necessary to overcome the despair of being unable to attain to truth, which is what their arguments seemed to lead one to. Among them every error is deemed a sin, and this can be warded off only by a systematic suspension of positive assent. Indeed they say it is an error if someone believes in what is uncertain. For them, however, nothing is certain in human experience, because of the deceitful likeness of falsehood to the truth, so that even if what appears to be true turns out to be true indeed, they will still dispute it with the most acute and even shameless arguments.

Among us, on the other hand, *"the righteous* [man] *shall live by his faith."*[39] Now, if you take away positive affirmation,[40] you take away faith, for without positive affirmation nothing is believed. And there are truths about things unseen, and unless they are believed, we cannot attain to

38. This refers to one of the first of the Cassiciacum dialogues, *Contra Academicos*. The gist of Augustine's refutation of skepticism is in 3:23ff. Throughout his whole career he continued to maintain this position: that certain knowledge begins with self-knowledge. See *Confessions*, book 5, chapter 10:19; see also *City of God*, 11:27.

39. Habakkuk 2:4 RSVCE.

40. A direct contrast between *suspensus assenso*—the watchword of the Academics—and *assensio*, the badge of Christian certitude.

the happy life, which is nothing less than life eternal. It is a question whether we ought to argue with those who profess themselves ignorant not only about the eternity yet to come but also about their present existence, for they (the academics) even argue that they do not know what they cannot help knowing. For no one can "not know" that he himself is alive. If he is not alive, he cannot "not know" about it or anything else at all, because either to know or to "not know" implies a living subject. But, in such a case, by not positively affirming that they are alive, the skeptics ward off the appearance of error in themselves, yet they do make errors simply by showing themselves alive; one cannot err who is not alive. That we live is therefore not only true, but it is altogether certain as well. And there are many things that are thus true and certain concerning which, if we withhold positive assent, this ought not to be regarded as a higher wisdom but actually a sort of dementia.

21. In those things which do not concern our attainment of the kingdom of God, it does not matter whether they are believed in or not, or whether they are true or are supposed to be true or false. To err in such questions, to mistake one thing for another, is not to be judged as a sin or, if it is, as a small and light one. In sum, whatever kind or how much of an error these miscues may be, it does not involve the way that leads to God, which is the faith of Christ that works through love. This way of life was not abandoned in that error so dear to parents concerning

the twins.[41] Nor did the apostle Peter deviate from this way when he thought he saw a vision and so mistook one thing for something else. In his case, he did not discover the actual situation until after the angel, by whom he was freed, had departed from him. Nor did the patriarch Jacob deviate from this way when he believed that his son, who was in fact alive, had been devoured by a wild beast. We may err through false impressions of this kind, with our faith in God still safe, nor do we thus leave the way that leads us to Him. Nevertheless, such mistakes, even if they are not sins, must still be listed among the evils of this life, which is so readily subject to vanity that we judge the false for true, reject the true for the false, and hold as uncertain what is actually certain. For even if these mistakes do not affect that faith by which we move forward to affirm truth and eternal beatitude, yet they are not unrelated to the misery in which we still exist. Actually, of course, we would be deceived in nothing at all, either in our souls or our physical senses, if we were already enjoying that true and perfected happiness.

22. Every lie, then, must be called a sin, because every man ought to speak what is in his heart—not only when he himself knows the truth, but even when he errs and is deceived, as a man may be. This is so whether it be true or is only supposed to be true when it is not. But a man who lies says the opposite of what is in his heart, with the deliberate intent to deceive. Now

41. See above, 7:90.

clearly, language, in its proper function, was developed not as a means whereby men could deceive one another, but as a medium through which a man could communicate his thought to others. Wherefore to use language in order to deceive, and not as it was designed to be used, is a sin.

Nor should we suppose that there is any such thing as a lie that is not a sin, just because we suppose that we can sometimes help somebody by lying. For we could also do this by stealing, as when a secret theft from a rich man who does not feel the loss is openly given to a pauper who greatly appreciates the gain. Yet no one would say that such a theft was not a sin. Or again, we could also "help" by committing adultery, if someone appeared to be dying for love if we would not consent to her desire and who, if she lived, might be purified by repentance. But it cannot be denied that such adultery would be a sin. If, then, we hold chastity in such high regard, wherein has truth offended us so that although chastity must not be violated by adultery, even for the sake of some other good, yet truth may be violated by lying? That men have made progress toward the good, when they will not lie save for the sake of human values, is not to be denied. But what is rightly praised in such a forward step, and perhaps even rewarded, is their good will and not their deceit. The deceit may be pardoned, but certainly ought not to be praised, especially among the heirs of the new covenant to whom it has been said,

"Let your communication be, Yea, yea; Nay, nay: for whatsoever is more than these cometh of evil."[42] Yet because of what this evil does, never ceasing to subvert this mortality of ours, even the joint heirs of Christ themselves pray, *"Forgive us our debts."*[43]

42. Matthew 5:37.
43. Matthew 6:12.

8

The Plight of Man After the Fall

23. With this much said, within the necessary brevity of this kind of treatise, as to what we need to know about the causes of good and evil—enough to lead us in the way toward the kingdom, where there will be life without death, truth without error, happiness without anxiety—we ought not to doubt in any way that the cause of everything pertaining to our good is nothing other than the bountiful goodness of God Himself. The cause of evil is the defection of the will of a being who is mutably good from the Good that is immutable. This happened first in the case of the angels and, afterward, that of man.

24. This was the primal lapse of the rational creature, that is, his first privation of the good. In train of this there crept in, even without his willing it, ignorance of the right things to do and also an appetite for noxious things. And these brought along with them, as their companions, error and misery. When these two evils are felt to be imminent, the soul's motion in flight from them is called fear.

Moreover, as the soul's appetites are satisfied by things harmful or at least inane—and as it fails to recognize the error of its ways—it falls victim to unwholesome pleasures or may even be exhilarated by vain joys. From these tainted springs of action—moved by the lash of appetite rather than a feeling of plenty—there flows out every kind of misery that is now the lot of rational natures.

25. Yet such a nature, even in its evil state, could not lose its appetite for blessedness. There are the evils that both men and angels have in common, for whose wickedness God has condemned them in simple justice. But man has a unique penalty as well: he is also punished by the death of the body. God had indeed threatened man with death as penalty if he should sin. He endowed him with freedom of the will in order that he might rule him by rational command and deter him by the threat of death. He even placed him in the happiness of paradise in a sheltered nook of life (*in umbra vitae*) where, by being a good steward of righteousness, he would rise to better things.

26. From this state, after he had sinned, man was banished, and through his sin he subjected his descendants to the punishment of sin and damnation, for he had radically corrupted them, in himself, by his sinning. As a consequence of this, all those descended from him and his wife (who had prompted him to sin and who was condemned along with him at the same time)—all those born through carnal lust, on whom the same penalty is visited as for disobedience—all these entered into the inheritance of original sin. Through this involvement they were led, through divers errors and sufferings (along with the rebel angels, their corruptors and possessors and companions), to that final stage of punishment without end. "*Wherefore, as by*

one man sin entered into the world, and death by sin; and so death passed upon all men, for that all have sinned."[44] By "the world" in this passage the apostle is, of course, referring to the whole human race.

27. This, then, was the situation: the whole mass of the human race stood condemned, lying ruined and wallowing in evil, being plunged from evil into evil and, having joined causes with the angels who had sinned, it was paying the fully deserved penalty for impious desertion. Certainly the anger of God rests, in full justice, on the deeds that the wicked do freely in blind and unbridled lust; and it is manifest in whatever penalties they are called on to suffer, both openly and secretly. Yet the Creator's goodness does not cease to sustain life and vitality even in the evil angels, for were this sustenance withdrawn, they would simply cease to exist. As for mankind, although born of a corrupted and condemned stock, he still retains the power to form and animate his seed, to direct his members in their temporal order, to enliven his senses in their spatial relations, and to provide bodily nourishment. For God judged it better to bring good out of evil than not to permit any evil to exist. And if He had willed that there should be no reformation in the case of men, as there is none for the wicked angels, would it not have been just if the nature that deserted God and, through the evil use of his powers, trampled and transgressed the precepts of his Creator, which could have been easily kept—the same creature

44. Romans 5:12.

who stubbornly turned away from His light and violated the image of the Creator in himself, who had in the evil use of his free will broken away from the wholesome discipline of God's law—would it not have been just if such a being had been abandoned by God wholly and forever and laid under the everlasting punishment that he deserved?

Clearly God would have done this if He were only just and not also merciful and if He had not willed to show far more striking evidence of His mercy by pardoning some who were unworthy of it.

9

The Replacement of the Fallen Angels By Elect Men (28–30); The Necessity of Grace (30–32)

28. While some of the angels deserted God in impious pride and were cast into the lowest darkness from the brightness of their heavenly home, the remaining number of the angels persevered in eternal bliss and holiness with God. For these faithful angels were not descended from a single angel, lapsed and damned. Hence, the original evil did not bind them in the fetters of inherited guilt, nor did it hand the whole company over to a deserved punishment, as is the human lot. Instead, when he who became the devil first rose in rebellion with his impious company and was then with them prostrated, the rest of the angels stood fast in pious obedience to the Lord and so received what the others had not had—a sure knowledge of their everlasting security in His unfailing steadfastness.

29. Thus it pleased God, Creator and Governor of the universe, that since the whole multitude of the angels had not perished in this desertion of him, those who had perished would remain forever in perdition, but those who had remained loyal through the revolt should go on rejoicing in the certain knowledge of the bliss forever theirs.

From the other part of the rational creation—that is, mankind—although it had perished as a whole through sins and punishments, both original and personal, God had determined that a portion of it would be restored and would fill up the loss which that diabolical disaster had caused in the angelic society. For this is the promise to the saints at the resurrection, that they shall be equal to the angels of God.[45]

Thus the heavenly Jerusalem, our mother and the commonwealth of God, shall not be defrauded of her full quota of citizens, but perhaps will rule over an even larger number. We know neither the number of holy men nor of the filthy demons, whose places are to be filled by the sons of the holy mother, who seemed barren in the earth, but whose sons will abide time without end in the peace the demons lost. But the number of those citizens, whether those who now belong or those who will in the future, is known to the mind of the Maker, who "*calleth those things which be not as though they were*"[46] and "ordered all things in measure and number and weight."[47]

30. But now, can that part of the human race to whom God promised deliverance and a place in the eternal kingdom be restored through the merits of their own works? Of course not! For what good works could a lost soul do except as he had been rescued from his lostness? Could

45. See Luke 20:36.

46. Romans 4:17.

47. Wisdom of Solomon 11:20 (Apocrypha).

he do this by the determination of his free will? Of course not! For it was in the evil use of his free will that man destroyed himself and his will at the same time. For as a man who kills himself is still alive when he kills himself, but having killed himself is then no longer alive and cannot resuscitate himself after he has destroyed his own life—so also sin which arises from the action of the free will turns out to be victor over the will and the free will is destroyed. *"Of whom a man is overcome, of the same is he brought in bondage."*[48] This is clearly the judgment of the apostle Peter. And since it is true, I ask you what kind of liberty can one have who is bound as a slave except the liberty that loves to sin?

He serves freely who freely does the will of his master. Accordingly he who is slave to sin is free to sin. But thereafter he will not be free to do right unless he is delivered from the bondage of sin and begins to be the servant of righteousness. This, then, is true liberty: the joy that comes in doing what is right. At the same time, it is also devoted service in obedience to righteous precept.

But how would a man, bound and sold, get back his liberty to do good, unless he could regain it from Him whose voice said, *"If the Son therefore shall make you free, ye shall be free indeed"*[49]? But before this process begins in man, could anyone glory in his good works as if they were acts of his free will, when he is not yet free to act rightly?

48. 2 Peter 2:19.
49. John 8:36.

He could do this only if, puffed up in proud vanity, he were merely boasting. This attitude is what the apostle was reproving when he said, *"By grace are ye saved through faith."*[50]

31. And lest men should arrogate to themselves saving faith as their own work and not understand it as a divine gift, the same apostle who says somewhere else that he had *"obtained mercy of the Lord to be faithful"*[51] makes here an additional comment: *"And that not of yourselves; it is the gift of God—not of works, lest any man should boast."*[52] But then, lest it be supposed that the faithful are lacking in good works, he added further, *"For we are his workmanship, created in Christ Jesus unto good works, which God hath before ordained that we should walk in them."*[53]

We are then truly free when God orders our lives, that is, forms and creates us not as men—this He has already done—but also as good men, which He is now doing by His grace, that we may indeed be new creatures in Christ Jesus.[54] Accordingly, the prayer: *"Create in me a clean heart, O God."*[55] This does not mean, as far as the natural human heart is concerned, that God has not already created this.

32. Once again, lest anyone glory, if not in his own works, at least in the determination of his free will, as if

50. Ephesians 2:8.
51. 1 Corinthians 7:25.
52. Ephesians 2:8–9.
53. Verse 10.
54. See Galatians 6:15; 2 Corinthians 5:17.
55. Psalm 51:10.

some merit had originated from him and as if the freedom to do good works had been bestowed on him as a kind of reward, let him hear the same herald of grace, announcing: "*For it is God which worketh in you both to will and to do of his good pleasure.*"[56] And, in another place: "*It is not of him that willeth, nor of him that runneth, but of God that sheweth mercy.*"[57] Still, it is obvious that a man who is old enough to exercise his reason cannot believe, hope, or love unless he wills it, nor could he run for the prize of his high calling in God without a decision of his will. In what sense, therefore, is it "not a matter of human willing or running but of God's showing mercy," unless it be that "the will itself is prepared by the Lord," even as it is written?[58]

This saying, therefore, that "*it is not of him that willeth, nor of him that runneth, but of God that sheweth mercy,*" means that the action is from both, that is to say, from the will of man and from the mercy of God. Thus we accept the dictum, "*It is not of him that willeth, nor of him that runneth, but of God that sheweth mercy,*" as if it meant, "The will of man is not sufficient by itself unless there is also the mercy of God." By the same token, the mercy of God is not sufficient by itself unless there is also the will of man. But if we say rightly that "*it is not of him that willeth, nor of him that runneth, but of God that sheweth mercy,*" because the will of man alone is not enough, why, then, is not the contrary rightly said, "It is not a matter of God's showing

56. Philippians 2:13.

57. Romans 9:16.

58. See Proverbs 8:35 (Septuagint translation).

mercy but of a man's willing," since the mercy of God by itself alone is not enough? Now, actually, no Christian would dare to say, "It is not a matter of God's showing mercy but of man's willing," lest he explicitly contradict the apostle. The conclusion remains, therefore, that this saying: "Not man's willing or running but God's showing mercy," is to be understood to mean that the whole process is credited to God, who both prepares the will to receive divine aid and aids the will that has been thus prepared.[59]

For a man's good will comes before many other gifts from God, but not all of them. One of the gifts it does not antedate is—just itself! Thus in the Sacred Eloquence we read both, "His mercy goes before me,"[60] and also, "His mercy shall follow me."[61] It predisposes a man before he wills, to prompt his willing. It follows the act of willing,

59. From the days at Cassiciacum till the very end, Augustine toiled with the mystery of the primacy of God's grace and the reality of human freedom. Of two things he was unwaveringly sure, even though they involved him in a paradox and the appearance of confusion. The first is that God's grace is not only primary but also sufficient as the ground and source of human willing. And against the Pelagians and other detractors from grace, he did not hesitate to insist that grace is irresistible and inviolable. See *On Grace and Free Will*, 99:41–43; *On the Predestination of the Saints*, 19:10; *On the Gift of Perseverance*, 41; *On the Soul and Its Origin*, 16; and even the Enchiridion, XXIV, 97.
But he never drew from this deterministic emphasis the conclusion that man is unfree and everywhere roundly rejects the not illogical corollary of his theonomism, that man's will counts for little or nothing except as passive agent of God's will. He insists on responsibility on man's part in responding to the initiatives of grace. For this emphasis, which is characteristically directed to the faithful themselves, see *On the Psalms*, 68:7-8; *Tractates on the Gospel of John*, 53:6-8; and even his severest anti-Pelagian tracts: *On Grace and Free Will*, 6-8, 10, 31 and *On Admonition and Grace*, 2-8.

60. Psalm 58:11 (Vulgate).

61. Cf. Psalm 23:6.

lest one's will be frustrated. Otherwise, why are we admonished to pray for our enemies,[62] who are plainly not now willing to live piously, unless it be that God is even now at work in them and in their wills?[63] Or again, why are we admonished to ask in order to receive, unless it be that He who grants us what we will is he through whom it comes to pass that we will? We pray for enemies, therefore, that the mercy of God should go before them, as it goes before us; we pray for ourselves that His mercy shall follow us.

---

62. See Matthew 5:44.
63. The theme that he had explored in Confessions, Books 1–9. See especially Book 5, Chapters 10, 13; Book 7, Chapter 8; Book 9, Chapter 1.

10

Jesus Christ the Mediator

33. Thus it was that the human race was bound in a just doom and all men were children of wrath. Of this wrath it is written: "For all our days are wasted; we are ruined in thy wrath; our years seem like a spider's web."[64] Likewise Job spoke of this wrath: "*Man that is born of a woman is of few days and full of trouble.*"[65] And even the Lord Jesus said of it: "*He that believeth on the Son hath everlasting life: and he that believeth not the Son shall not see life; but the wrath of God abideth on him.*"[66] He does not say, "It will come," but, "It now abides." Indeed every man is born into this state. Wherefore the apostle says, "[For we too] *were by nature the children of wrath, even as others.*"[67] Since men are in this state of wrath through original sin—a condition made still graver and more pernicious as they compounded more and worse sins with it—a Mediator was required; that is to say, a Reconciler who by offering a unique sacrifice, of which all the sacrifices of the law and the prophets were shadows, should allay that wrath. Thus the apostle says, "*For if, when we were enemies, we were reconciled to God by the death of his Son, much more, being reconciled, we*

64. See Psalm 90:9.
65. Job 14:1.
66. John 3:36.
67. Ephesians 2:3.

shall be saved by his life."[68] However, when God is said to be wrathful, this does not signify any such perturbation in Him as there is in the soul of a wrathful man. His verdict, which is always just, takes the name "wrath" as a term borrowed from the language of human feelings. This, then, is the grace of God through Jesus Christ our Lord—that we are reconciled to God through the Mediator and receive the Holy Spirit so that we may be changed from enemies into sons, *"for as many as are led by the Spirit of God, they are the sons of God."*[69]

34. It would take too long to say all that would be truly worthy of this Mediator. Indeed, men cannot speak properly of such matters. For who can unfold in cogent enough fashion this statement, that *"the Word was made flesh and dwelt among us,"*[70] so that we should then believe in "the only Son of God the Father Almighty, born of the Holy Spirit and Mary the Virgin." Yet it is indeed true that the Word was made flesh, the flesh being assumed by the Divinity, not the Divinity being changed into flesh. Of course, by the term "flesh" we ought here to understand "man," an expression in which the part signifies the whole, just as it is said, *"Therefore by the deeds of the law shall no flesh be justified,"*[71] which is to say, no man shall be justified. Yet certainly we must say that in that assumption nothing was lacking that belongs to human nature.

68. Romans 5:10.

69. Romans 8:14.

70. John 1:14.

71. Romans 3:20.

But it was a nature entirely free from the bonds of all sin. It was not a nature born of both sexes with fleshly desires, with the burden of sin, the guilt of which is washed away in regeneration. Instead, it was the kind of nature that would be fittingly born of a virgin, conceived by His mother's faith and not her fleshly desires. Now if in His being born, her virginity had been destroyed, He would not then have been born of a virgin. It would then be false (which is unthinkable) for the whole church to confess Him "born of the Virgin Mary." This is the church which, imitating His mother, daily gives birth to His members yet remains virgin. Read, if you please, my letter on the virginity of Saint Mary written to that illustrious man, Volusianus, whom I name with honor and affection.[72]

35. Christ Jesus, Son of God, is thus both God and man. He was God before all ages; He is man in this age of ours. He is God because He is the Word of God, for "*the Word was God.*"[73] Yet He is man also, since in the unity of his person a rational soul and body is joined to the Word.

Accordingly, in so far as He is God, He and the Father are one. Yet in so far as He is man, the Father is greater than He. Since He was God's only Son—not by grace but by nature—to the end that He might indeed be the fullness of all grace, He was also made Son of Man—and yet He was in the one nature as well as in the other,

72. Epistle 137, written in 412 in reply to a list of queries sent to Augustine by the proconsul of Africa.
73. John 1:1.

one Christ. "*Who, being in the form of God, thought it not robbery to be equal with God: but made himself of no reputation, and took upon him the form of a servant*"[74] yet neither losing nor diminishing the form of God.[75] Thus He was made less and remained equal, and both these in a unity as we said before. But He is one of these because He is the Word; the other, because He was a man. As the Word, He is the equal of the Father; as a man, He is less. He is the one Son of God, and at the same time Son of Man; the one Son of Man, and at the same time God's Son. These are not two sons of God, one God and the other man, but one Son of God—God without origin, man with a definite origin—our Lord Jesus Christ.

74. Philippians 2:6–7.
75. These metaphors for contrasting the "two natures" of Jesus Christ were favorite figures of speech in Augustine's Christological thought. Cf. *On the Gospel of John,* Tractate 78; *On the Trinity,* 1:7; 2:2; 4:19-20; 7:3; New Testament Sermons, 76, 14.

11

The Incarnation as Prime Example of the Action of God's Grace

36. In this the grace of God is supremely manifest, commended in grand and visible fashion; for what had the human nature in the man Christ merited, that it, and no other, should be assumed into the unity of the person of the only Son of God? What good will, what zealous strivings, what good works preceded this assumption by which that particular man deserved to become one person with God? Was He a man before the union, and was this singular grace given him as to one particularly deserving before God? Of course not! For, from the moment He began to be a man, that man began to be nothing other than God's Son, the only Son, and this because the Word of God assuming Him became flesh, yet still assuredly remained God. Just as every man is a personal unity—that is, a unity of rational soul and flesh—so also is Christ a personal unity: Word and man.

Why should there be such great glory to a human nature—and this undoubtedly an act of grace, no merit preceding unless it be that those who consider such a question faithfully and soberly might have here a clear manifestation of God's great and sole grace, and this in order that they might understand how they themselves are justified from their sins by the selfsame grace that made it so that the man Christ had no power to sin? Thus indeed the angel hailed His mother when announcing to her the future birth: "Hail," he said, "full of grace."[76] And shortly thereafter, *"Thou hast found favour with God."*[77] And this was said of her, that she was full of grace, since she was to be mother of her Lord, indeed the Lord of all. Yet, concerning Christ Himself, when the evangelist John said, *"And the Word became flesh and dwelt among us,"* he added, *"and we beheld his glory, a glory as of the only Son of the Father, full of grace and truth."*[78] When he said, *"The Word was made flesh,"* this means, "Full of grace." When he also said, *"The glory as of the only begotten of the Father,"* this means, "Full of truth." Indeed it was truth Himself, God's only begotten Son—and, again, this not by grace but by nature—who, by grace, assumed human nature into such a personal unity that He Himself became the Son of Man as well.

37. This same Jesus Christ, God's one and only Son our Lord, was born of the Holy Spirit and the Virgin Mary. Now obviously the Holy Spirit is God's gift, a gift that is itself equal to the Giver; wherefore the Holy Spirit is God also, not inferior to the Father and the Son. Now what does this mean, that Christ's birth in respect to His

76. Luke 1:28 (Vulgate).
77. Luke 1:30.
78. John 1:14.

human nature was of the Holy Spirit, save that this was itself also a work of grace?

For when the Virgin asked of the angel the manner by which what he announced would come to pass (since she had known no man), the angel answered: "*The Holy Ghost shall come upon thee, and the power of the Highest shall overshadow thee: therefore also that holy thing which shall be born of thee shall be called the Son of God.*"[79] And when Joseph wished to put her away, suspecting adultery (since he knew she was not pregnant by him), he received a similar answer from the angel: "*Fear not to take unto thee Mary thy wife: for that which is conceived in her is of the Holy Ghost*"[80]—that is, "What you suspect is from another man is of the Holy Spirit."

79. Luke 1:35.
80. Matthew 1:20.

12

The Role of the Holy Spirit

38. Are we, then, to say that the Holy Spirit is the Father of Christ's human nature, so that as God the Father generated the Word, so the Holy Spirit generated the human nature, and that from both natures Christ came to be one, Son of God the Father as the Word, Son of the Holy Spirit as man? Do we suppose that the Holy Spirit is His Father through begetting Him of the Virgin Mary? Who would dare to say such a thing? There is no need to show by argument how many absurd consequences such a notion has, when it is so absurd in itself that no believer's ear can bear to hear it. Actually, then, as we confess our Lord Jesus Christ, who is God from God yet born as man of the Holy Spirit and the Virgin Mary, there is in each nature (in both the divine and the human) the only Son of God the Father Almighty, from whom proceeds the Holy Spirit.

How, then, do we say that Christ is born of the Holy Spirit, if the Holy Spirit did not beget Him? Is it because he made Him? This might be, since through our Lord Jesus Christ—in the form of God—all things were made. Yet in so far as He is man, He Himself was made, even as the apostle says: "[He] *was made of the seed of David according to the flesh."*[81] But since that creature that the Virgin conceived and bore, though it was related to the person of the Son alone, was made by the whole Trinity—for the works of the Trinity are not separable—why is the Holy Spirit named as the One who made it? Is it, perhaps, that when any One of the Three is named in connection with some divine action, the whole Trinity is to be understood as involved in that action? This is true and can be shown by examples, but we should not dwell too long on this kind of solution.

For what still concerns us is how it can be said, *"Born of the Holy Spirit,"* when He is in no wise the Son of the Holy Spirit? Now, just because God made (*fecit*) this world, one could not say that the world is the son of God, or that it is "born" of God. Rather, one says it was "made" or "created" or "founded" or "established" by Him, or however else one might like to speak of it. So, then, when we confess, "Born of the Holy Spirit and the Virgin Mary," the sense in which He is not the Son of the Holy Spirit and yet is the son of the Virgin Mary, when He was born both of Him and of her, is difficult to explain. But there is no doubt as to the fact that He was not born from Him as Father as He was born of her as mother.

39. Consequently we should not grant that whatever is born of something should therefore be called the son of that thing. Let us pass over the fact that a son is "born" of a man in a different sense than a hair is, or a louse, or a

81. Romans 1:3.

maw worm—none of these is a son. Let us pass over these things, since they are an unfitting analogy in so great a matter. Yet it is certain that those who are born of water and of the Holy Spirit would not properly be called sons of the water by anyone. But it does make sense to call them sons of God the Father and of mother church. Thus, therefore, the one born of the Holy Spirit is the son of God the Father, not of the Holy Spirit.

What we said about the hair and the other things has this much relevance, that it reminds us that not everything that is "born" of something is said to be "son" to Him from which it is "born." Likewise, it does not follow that those who are called sons of someone are always said to have been born of Him, since there are some who are adopted. Even those who are called "sons of Gehenna" are not born of it, but have been destined for it, just as the sons of the kingdom are destined for that.

40. Wherefore, since a thing may be "born" of something else, yet not in the fashion of a "son," and conversely, since not everyone who is called son is born of Him whose son he is called—this is the very mode in which Christ was "born" of the Holy Spirit (yet not as a son), and of the Virgin Mary as a son—this suggests to us the grace of God by which a certain human person, no merit whatever preceding, at the very outset of his existence, was joined to the Word of God in such a unity of person that the selfsame one who is Son of Man should be Son of God, and the one who is Son of God should be Son of Man. Thus,

in His assumption of human nature, grace came to be natural to that nature, allowing no power to sin. This is why grace is signified by the Holy Spirit, because He Himself is so perfectly God that He is also called God's Gift. Still, to speak adequately of this—even if one could—would call for a very long discussion.

13

Baptism and Original Sin

41. Since He was begotten and conceived in no pleasure of carnal appetite—and therefore bore no trace of original sin—He was, by the grace of God (operating in a marvelous and an ineffable manner), joined and united in a personal unity with the only-begotten Word of the Father, a Son not by grace but by nature. And although He Himself committed no sin, yet because of "*the likeness of sinful flesh*"[82] in which He came, He was Himself called sin and was made a sacrifice for the washing away of sins.

Indeed, under the old law, sacrifices for sins were often called sins.[83] Yet He of whom those sacrifices were mere shadows was Himself actually made sin. Thus, when the apostle said, "*Now then we are ambassadors for Christ, as though God did beseech you by us,*" he straightway added, "*For He hath made Him to be sin for us that we might be made the righteousness of God in him.*"[84] He does not say, as we read in some defective copies, "He who knew no sin did sin for us," as if Christ himself committed sin for our sake. Rather, he says, "*He* [God] *hath made him* [Christ] *to be sin for us, who knew no sin.*" The God to whom we are to

82. Romans 8:3.
83. See Hosea 4:8.
84. 2 Corinthians 5:21.

be reconciled hath thus made Him the sacrifice for sin by which we may be reconciled.

He Himself is therefore sin as we ourselves are righteousness—not our own but God's, not in ourselves but in Him. Just as He was sin—not His own but ours, rooted not in Himself but in us—so He showed forth through the likeness of sinful flesh, in which He was crucified, that since sin was not in Him He could then, so to say, die to sin by dying in the flesh, which was "the likeness of sin." And since He had never lived in the old manner of sinning, He might, in His resurrection, signify the new life which is ours, which is springing to life anew from the old death in which we had been dead to sin.

42. This is the meaning of the great sacrament of baptism, which is celebrated among us. All who attain to this grace die thereby to sin—as He Himself is said to have died to sin because He died in the flesh, that is, "in the likeness of sin"—and they are thereby alive by being reborn in the baptismal font, just as he rose again from the sepulcher. This is the case no matter what the age of the body.

43. For whether it be a newborn infant or a decrepit old man—since no one should be barred from baptism—just so, there is no one who does not die to sin in baptism. Infants die to original sin only; adults, to all those sins that they have added, through their evil living, to the burden they brought with them at birth.

44. But even these are frequently said to die to sin, when without doubt they die not to one but to many sins, and to all the sins that they have themselves already committed by thought, word, and deed. Actually, by the use of the singular number the plural number is often signified, as the poet said, "And they fill the belly with the armed warrior,"[85] although they did this with many warriors. And in our own Scriptures we read: *"Pray unto the LORD, that he take away the serpents from us."*[86] It does not say "serpents," as it might, for they were suffering from many serpents. There are, moreover, innumerable other such examples.

Yet, when the original sin is signified by the use of the plural number, as we say when infants are baptized "unto the remission of sins," instead of saying "unto the remission of sin," then we have the converse expression in which the singular is expressed by the plural number. Thus in the gospel, it is said of Herod's death, *"For they are dead which sought the young child's life"*[87]; it does not say, "He is dead." And in Exodus: *"The people...have made,"* [Moses] says, *"them gods of gold,"*[88] when they had made one calf. And of this calf, they said: *"These be thy gods, O Israel, which have brought thee up out of the land of Egypt,"*[89] here also putting the plural for the singular.

85. Virgil, *Aeneid,* 2:1, 20.
86. Numbers 21:7.
87. Matthew 2:20.
88. Exodus 32:31.
89. Verse 8.

45. Still, even in that one sin—which "entered into the world by one man and so spread to all men,"[90] and on account of which infants are baptized—one can recognize a plurality of sins, if that single sin is divided, so to say, into its separate elements. For there is pride in it, since man preferred to be under his own rule rather than the rule of God; and sacrilege too, for man did not acknowledge God; and murder, since He cast Himself down to death; and spiritual fornication, for the integrity of the human mind was corrupted by the seduction of the serpent; and theft, since the forbidden fruit was snatched; and avarice, since he hungered for more than should have sufficed for him—and whatever other sins that could be discovered in the diligent analysis of that one sin.

46. It is also said—and not without support—that infants are involved in the sins of their parents, not only of the first pair, but even of their own, of whom they were born. Indeed, that divine judgment, *"visiting the iniquities of the fathers upon the children,"*[91] definitely applies to them before they come into the new covenant by regeneration. This covenant was foretold by Ezekiel when he said that the sons should not bear their fathers' sins, nor the proverb any longer apply in Israel, *"The fathers have eaten sour grapes, and the children's teeth are set on edge."*[92]

90. See Romans 5:12.
91. Deuteronomy 5:9.
92. Ezekiel 18:2.

This is why each one of them must be born again, so that he may thereby be absolved of whatever sin was in him at the time of birth. For the sins committed by evil-doing after birth can be healed by repentance—as, indeed, we see it happen even after baptism. For the new birth (*regeneratio*) would not have been instituted except for the fact that the first birth (*generatio*) was tainted—and to such a degree that one born of even a lawful wedlock said, "I was conceived in iniquities; and in sins did my mother conceive me."[93] Nor did he say "in iniquity" or "in sin," as he might have quite correctly; rather, he preferred to say "iniquities" and "sins," because, as I explained above, there are so many sins in that one sin—which has passed into all men, and which was so great that human nature was changed and by it brought under the necessity of death—and also because there are other sins, such as those of parents, which, even if they cannot change our nature in the same way, still involve the children in guilt, unless the gracious grace and mercy of God interpose.

47. But, in the matter of the sins of one's other parents, those who stand as one's forebears from Adam down to one's own parents, a question might well be raised: whether a man at birth is involved in the evil deeds of all his forebears, and their multiplied original sins, so that the later in time he is born, the worse estate he is born in; or whether, on this very account, God threatens to visit the sins of the parents as far as—but no farther than—the

93. Psalm 50:7 (Vulgate).

third and fourth generations, because in His mercy He will not continue His wrath beyond that. It is not His purpose that those not given the grace of regeneration be crushed under too heavy a burden in their eternal damnation, as they would be if they were bound to bear, as original guilt, all the sins of their ancestors from the beginning of the human race, and to pay the due penalty for them. Whether yet another solution to so difficult a problem might or might not be found by a more diligent search and interpretation of Holy Scripture, I dare not rashly affirm.

14

The Mysteries of Christ's Mediatorial Work (48–49) and Justification (50–55)

48. That one sin, however, committed in a setting of such great happiness, was itself so great that by it, in one man, the whole human race was originally and, so to say, radically condemned. It cannot be pardoned and washed away except through the *"one mediator between God and men, the man Christ Jesus,"*[94] who alone could be born in such a way as not to need to be reborn.

49. They were not reborn, those who were baptized by John's baptism, by which Christ Himself was baptized.[95] Rather, they were prepared by the ministry of this forerunner, who said, *"Prepare ye the way of the Lord,"*[96] for Him in whom alone they could be reborn.

For His baptism is not with water alone, as John's was, but with the Holy Spirit as well. Thus, whoever believes in Christ is reborn by that same Spirit, of whom Christ also was born, needing not to be reborn. This is the reason for the voice of the Father spoken over Him at his baptism, *"To day have I begotten thee,"*[97] which pointed not to

94. 1 Timothy 2:5.

95. See Matthew 3:13.

96. Luke 3:4; see also Isaiah 40:3.

97. Hebrews 5:5; see also Mark 1:9–11.

that particular day on which He was baptized, but to that "day" of changeless eternity, in order to show us that this Man belonged to the personal unity of the Only Begotten. For a day that neither begins with the close of yesterday nor ends with the beginning of tomorrow is indeed an eternal "today."

Therefore, He chose to be baptized in water by John, not thereby to wash away any sin of His own, but to manifest His great humility. Indeed, baptism found nothing in Him to wash away, just as death found nothing to punish. Hence, it was in authentic justice, and not by violent power, that the devil was overcome and conquered: for, as he had most unjustly slain Him who was in no way deserving of death, He also did most justly lose those whom he had justly held in bondage as punishment for their sins. Wherefore, He took upon Himself both baptism and death, not out of a piteous necessity but through His own free act of showing mercy—as part of a definite plan whereby One might take away the sin of the world, just as one man had brought sin into the world, that is, the whole human race.

50. There is a difference, however. The first man brought sin into the world, whereas this One took away not only that one sin but also all the others that he found added to it. Hence, the apostle says, *"And the free gift* [of grace] *is not like the effect of that one man's sin. For the judgment following one trespass brought condemnation; but the*

free gift following many trespasses brings justification."[98] Now it is clear that the one sin originally inherited, even if it were the only one involved, makes men liable to condemnation. Yet grace justifies a man for many offenses, both the sin that he originally inherited in common with all the others and also the multitude of sins that he has committed on his own.

51. However, when he (the apostle) says, shortly after, *"Therefore as by the offense of one judgment came upon all men to condemnation; even so by the righteousness of one the free gift came upon all men unto justification of life"*[99] he indicates sufficiently that everyone born of Adam is subject to damnation, and no one, unless reborn of Christ, is free from such a damnation.

52. And after this discussion of punishment through one man and grace through the Other, as he deemed sufficient for that part of the epistle, the apostle passes on to speak of the great mystery of holy baptism in the cross of Christ, and to do this so that we may understand nothing other in the baptism of Christ than the likeness of the death of Christ. The death of Christ crucified is nothing other than the likeness of the forgiveness of sins—so that in the very same sense in which the death is real, so also is the forgiveness of our sins real, and in the same sense in which His resurrection is real, so also in us is there authentic justification.

98. Romans 5:16 RSVCE.

99. Romans 5:18.

He asks: *"What shall we say then? Shall we continue in sin, that grace may abound?"*[100]—for he had previously said, *"But where sin abounded, grace did much more abound."*[101] And therefore he himself raised the question whether, because of the abundance of grace that follows sin, one should then continue in sin. But he answers, *"God forbid,"* and adds, *"How shall we, that are dead to sin, live any longer therein?"*[102] Then, to show that we are dead to sin, *"Know ye not, that so many of us as were baptized into Jesus Christ were baptized into his death?"*[103]

If, therefore, the fact that we are baptized into the death of Christ shows that we are dead to sin, then certainly infants who are baptized in Christ die to sin, since they are baptized into His own death. For there is no exception in the saying, "All we who are baptized into Christ Jesus are baptized into His death." And the effect of this is to show that we are dead to sin.

Yet what sin do infants die to in being reborn except that which they inherit in being born? What follows in the epistle also pertains to this:

> *Therefore we are buried with him by baptism into death: that like as Christ was raised up from the dead by the glory of the Father, even so we also should walk in newness of life. For if we have been planted*

100. Romans 6:1.
101. Romans 5:20.
102. Romans 6:2.
103. Verse 3.

together in the likeness of his death, we shall be also in the likeness of his resurrection: knowing this, that our old man is crucified with him, that the body of sin might be destroyed, that henceforth we should not serve sin. For he that is dead is freed from sin. Now if we be dead with Christ, we believe that we shall also live with him: knowing that Christ being raised from the dead dieth no more; death hath no more dominion over him. For in that he died, he died unto sin once: but in that he liveth, he liveth unto God. Likewise reckon ye also yourselves to be dead indeed unto sin, but alive unto God through Jesus Christ our Lord.[104]

Now, he had set out to prove that we should not go on sinning, in order that thereby grace might abound, and had said, "If we have died to sin, how, then, shall we go on living in it?" And then to show that we were dead to sin, he had added, *"Know ye not, that so many of us as were baptized into Jesus Christ were baptized into his death?"*[105] Thus he concludes the passage as he began it. Indeed, he introduced the death of Christ in order to say that even he died to sin. To what sin, save that of the flesh in which he existed, not as sinner, but in "the likeness of sin" and that was, therefore, called by the name of sin? Thus, to those baptized into the death of Christ—into which not only

104. Verses 4–11.
105. Verse 3.

adults but infants as well are baptized—he says, *"Reckon ye also yourselves to be dead unto sin, but alive unto God through Jesus Christ our Lord."*[106]

53. Whatever was done, therefore, in the crucifixion of Christ, His burial, His resurrection on the third day, His ascension into heaven, His being seated at the Father's right hand—all these things were done thus, that they might not only signify their mystical meanings but also serve as a model for the Christian life that we lead here on the earth. Thus, of his crucifixion it was said, *"And they that are Christ's have crucified the flesh with the affections and lusts"*[107]; and of his burial, *"For we are buried with* [Christ] *by baptism into death:"*—of his resurrection—*"that like as Christ was raised up from the dead through the glory of the Father, even so we should walk in newness of life"*[108]; of His ascension and session at the Father's right hand:

> *If ye then be risen with Christ, seek those things which are above, where Christ sitteth on the right hand of God. Set your affection on things above, not on things on the earth. For ye are dead, and your life is hid with Christ in God.*[109]

54. Now what we believe concerning Christ's future actions, since we confess that He will come again from

106. Verse 11.
107. Galatians 5:24.
108. Romans 6:4.
109. Colossians 3:1–3.

heaven to judge the living and the dead, does not pertain to this life of ours as we live it here on earth, because it belongs not to His deeds already done, but to what He will do at the close of the age. To this the apostle refers and goes on to add, *"When Christ, who is our life, shall appear, then shall ye also appear with him in glory."*[110]

55. There are two ways to interpret the affirmation that He "shall judge the living and the dead." On the one hand, we may understand by "the living" those who are not yet dead but who will be found living in the flesh when He comes; and we may understand by "the dead" those who have left the body, or who shall have left it before His coming. Or, on the other hand, "the living" may signify "the righteous," and "the dead" may signify "the unrighteous"—since the righteous are to be judged as well as the unrighteous. For sometimes the judgment of God is passed upon the evil, as in the word, *"and they that have done evil,* [shall come forth] *unto the resurrection of damnation."*[111] And sometimes it is passed upon the good, as in the word, *"Save me, O God, by thy name, and judge me by thy strength."*[112] Indeed, it is by the judgment of God that the distinction between good and evil is made, to the end that, being freed from evil and not destroyed with the evildoers, the good may be set apart at His right hand.[113]

---

110. Verse 4.
111. John 5:29.
112. Psalm 54:1.
113. See Matthew 25:32–33.

This is why the psalmist cried, *"Judge me, O God,"* and, as if to explain what He had said, *"and plead my cause against an ungodly nation."*[114]

114. Psalm 43:1.

15

The Holy Spirit (56) and the Church (57–60)

56. Now, when we have spoken of Jesus Christ, the only Son of God our Lord, in the brevity befitting our confession of faith, we go on to affirm that we believe also in the Holy Spirit, as completing the Trinity that is God; and after that we call to mind our faith "in holy church." By this we are given to understand that the rational creation belonging to the free Jerusalem ought to be mentioned in a subordinate order to the Creator, that is, the supreme Trinity. For, of course, all that has been said about the man Christ Jesus refers to the unity of the Person of the Only Begotten. Thus, the right order of the Creed demanded[115] that the church be made subordinate to the Trinity, as a house is subordinate to Him who dwells in it, the temple to God, and the city to its founder. By the church here we are to understand the whole church, not just the part that journeys here on earth from rising of the sun to its setting, praising the name of the Lord[116] and singing a new song of deliverance from its old captivity, but also that part which, in heaven, has always, from creation, held fast to God, and which never experienced the evils of a fall. This

115. Reading the classical Latin form *poscebat* (as in Scheel and PL) for the late form *poxebat* (as in Rivière and many old MSS.).
116. See Psalm 113:3.

part, composed of the holy angels, remains in blessedness, and it gives help, even as it ought, to the other part still on pilgrimage. For both parts together will make one eternal consort, as even now they are one in the bond of love—the whole instituted for the proper worship of the one God.[117]

Wherefore, neither the whole church nor any part of it wishes to be worshiped as God nor to be God to anyone belonging to the temple of God—the temple that is being built up of "the gods" whom the uncreated God created.[118] Consequently, if the Holy Spirit were creature and not Creator, he would obviously be a rational creature, for this is the highest of the levels of creation. But in this case He would not be set in the rule of faith before the church, since He would then belong to the church, in that part of it that is in heaven. He would not have a temple, for He Himself would be a temple. Yet, in fact, He hath a temple of which the apostle speaks, *"Know ye not that your body is the temple of the Holy Ghost which is in you, which ye have of God…?"*[119] In another place, he says of this body, *"Know ye not that your bodies are members of Christ?"*[120] How, then, is He not God who has a temple? Or how can He be less than Christ whose members are His temple? It is not that He has one temple and God another temple, since the same apostle says: *"Know ye not that ye are the temple of*

117. Here reading *unum deum* (with Rivière and PL) against *deum* (in Scheel).
118. A hyperbolic expression referring to "the saints." Augustine's Scriptural backing for such an unusual phrase is Psalm 82:6 and John 10:34. But note the firm distinction between *ex diis quos facit* and *non factus Deus*.
119. 1 Corinthians 6:19.
120. Verse 15.

God," and then, as if to prove his point, added, *"and that the Spirit of God dwelleth in you?"*[121]

God therefore dwells in His temple, not the Holy Spirit only, but also Father and Son, who says of His body—in which He stands as Head of the church on earth *"that in all things he might have the preeminence"*[122]—*"Destroy this temple, and in three days I will raise it up."*[123] Therefore, the temple of God—that is, of the supreme Trinity as a whole—is holy church, the universal church in heaven and on the earth.

57. But what can we affirm about that part of the church in heaven, save that in it no evil is to be found, nor any apostates, nor will there be again, since that time when *"God spared not the angels that sinned"*—as the apostle Peter writes—*"but cast them down to hell, and delivered them into chains of darkness, to be reserved unto judgment"*[124]?

58. Still, how is life ordered in that most blessed and supernal society? What differences are there in rank among the angels, so that while all are called by the general title "angels"—as we read in the Epistle to the Hebrews, *"But to which of the angels said he at any time, Sit at my right hand...?"*[125]; this expression clearly signifies that all are angels without exception—yet there are archangels there as well? Again, should these archangels be called

121. 1 Corinthians 3:16.
122. Colossians 1:18.
123. John 2:19.
124. 2 Peter 2:4.
125. Hebrews 1:13.

"powers" (*virtutes*), so that the verse, *"Praise ye him, all his angels; praise ye him, all his hosts,"*[126] would mean the same thing as, "Praise Him, all His angels; praise Him, all His archangels"? Or, what distinctions are implied by the four designations by which the apostle seems to encompass the entire heavenly society, *"whether they be thrones, or dominions, or principalities, or powers"*[127]? Let them answer these questions who can, if they can indeed prove their answers. For myself, I confess to ignorance of such matters. I am not even certain about another question: whether the sun and moon and all the stars belong to that same heavenly society—although they seem to be nothing more than luminous bodies, with neither perception nor understanding.

59. Furthermore, who can explain the kind of bodies in which the angels appeared to men, so that they were not only visible, but tangible as well? And, again, how do they, not by impact of physical stimulus but by spiritual force, bring certain visions, not to the physical eyes but to the spiritual eyes of the mind, or speak something, not to the ears, as from outside us, but actually from within the human soul, since they are present within it too? For, as it is written in the book of the prophets: *"And the angel that talked with me said unto me...."*[128] He does not say "talked to me" but *"talked with me."* How do they appear to men in sleep, and communicate through dreams, as we read in the gospel: *"Behold, the angel of the Lord appeared unto him*

126. Psalm 148:2.
127. Colossians 1:16.
128. Zechariah 1:9.

in a dream, saying,,,,”[129]? By these various modes of presentation, the angels seem to indicate that they do not have tangible bodies. Yet this raises a very difficult question: How, then, did the patriarchs wash the angels' feet?[130] How, also, did Jacob wrestle with the angel in such a tangible fashion?[131]

To ask such questions as these, and to guess at the answers as one can, is not a useless exercise in speculation, so long as the discussion is moderate and one avoids the mistake of those who think they know what they do not know.

129. Matthew 1:20.
130. See Genesis 18:4; 19:2.
131. See Genesis 32:24.

11

Problems About Heavenly and Earthly Divisions of the Church

60. It is more important to be able to discern and tell when Satan transforms himself as an angel of light, lest by this deception he should seduce us into harmful acts. For, when he deceives the corporeal senses, and does not thereby turn the mind from that true and right judgment by which one leads the life of faith, there is no danger to religion. Or if, feigning himself to be good, he does or says things that would fit the character of the good angels, even if then we believe him good, the error is neither dangerous nor fatal to the Christian faith. But when, by these alien wiles, he begins to lead us into his own ways, then great vigilance is required to recognize him and not follow after. But how few men are there who are able to avoid his deadly stratagems, unless God guides and preserves them! Yet the very difficulty of this business is useful in this respect: it shows that no man should rest his hopes in himself, nor one man in another, but all who are God's should cast their hopes on Him. And that this latter is obviously the best course for us no pious man would deny.

61. This part of the church, therefore, which is composed of the holy angels and powers of God will become

known to us as it really is only when, at the end of the age, we are joined to it, to possess, together with it, eternal bliss. But the other part which, separated from this heavenly company, wanders through the earth is better known to us because we are in it, and because it is composed of men like ourselves. This is the part that has been redeemed from all sin by the blood of the sinless Mediator, and its cry is: *"If God be for us, who can be against us? He that spared not his own Son, but delivered him up for us all."*[132] Now Christ did not die for the angels. But still, what was done for man by His death for man's redemption and His deliverance from evil was done for the angels also, because by it the enmity caused by sin between men and the angels is removed and friendship restored. Moreover, this redemption of mankind serves to repair the ruins left by the angelic apostasy.

62. Of course, the holy angels, taught by God—in the eternal contemplation of whose truth they are blessed—know how many of the human race are required to fill up the full census of that commonwealth. This is why the apostle says *"that in the dispensation of the fulness of times he might gather together in one all things in Christ, both which are in heaven, and which are on earth, even in him."*[133] The part in heaven is indeed restored when the number lost from the angelic apostasy are replaced from the ranks of mankind. The part on earth is restored when those men

132. Romans 8:31–32.
133. Ephesians 1:10.

predestined to eternal life are redeemed from the old state of corruption.

Thus by the single sacrifice, of which the many victims of the law were only shadows, the heavenly part is set at peace with the earthly part and the earthly reconciled to the heavenly. Wherefore, as the same apostle says:

> *For it pleased the Father that in him should all fulness dwell; and, having made peace through the blood of his cross, by him to reconcile all things unto himself; by him, I say, whether they be things in earth, or things in heaven.*[134]

63. This peace, as it is written, "*passeth all understanding.*"[135] It cannot be known by us until we have entered into it. For how is the heavenly realm set at peace, save together with us; that is, by concord with us? For in that realm there is always peace, both among the whole company of rational creatures and between them and their Creator. This is the peace that, as it is said, "*passeth all understanding.*" But obviously this means our understanding, not that of those who always see the Father's face. For no matter how great our understanding may be, "*Now we see through a glass, darkly;...now* [we] *know in part*"[136] But when we shall have become "*equal unto the angels,*"[137] then, even as they do, "we

134. Colossians 1:19–20.
135. Philippians 4:7.
136. 1 Corinthians 13:12.
137. Luke 20:36.

shall see face to face."[138] And we shall then have as great amity toward them as they have toward us; for we shall come to love them as much as we are loved by them.

In this way their peace will become known to us, since ours will be like theirs in kind and measure—nor will it then surpass our understanding. But the peace of God, which is there, will still doubtless surpass our understanding and theirs as well. For, of course, in so far as a rational creature is blessed, this blessedness comes, not from himself, but from God. Hence, it follows that it is better to interpret the passage, "*The peace of God which passeth all understanding,*" so that from the word "*all*" not even the understanding of the holy angels should be excepted. Only God's understanding is excepted; for, of course, His peace does not surpass His own understanding.

138. See 1 Corinthians 13:12.

17

Forgiveness of Sins in the Church

64. The angels are in concord with us even now, when our sins are forgiven. Therefore, in the order of the Creed, after the reference to "holy church" is placed the reference to "forgiveness of sins." For it is by this that the part of the church on earth stands; it is by this that "what was lost and is found again"[139] is not lost again. Of course, the gift of baptism is an exception. It is an antidote given us against original sin, so that what is contracted by birth is removed by the new birth—though it also takes away actual sins as well, whether of heart, word, or deed. But except for this great remission—the beginning point of a man's renewal, in which all guilt, inherited and acquired, is washed away—the rest of life, from the age of accountability (and no matter how vigorously we progress in righteousness), is not without the need for the forgiveness of sins.

This is the case because the sons of God, as long as they live this mortal life, are in a conflict with death. And although it is truly said of them, *"As many as are led by the Spirit of God, they are the sons of God,"*[140] yet even as they are being led by the Spirit of God and, as sons

139. See Luke 15:24.
140. Romans 8:14.

of God, advance toward God, they are also being led by their own spirits so that, weighed down by the corruptible body and influenced by certain human feelings, they thus fall away from themselves and commit sin. But it matters how much. Although every crime is a sin, not every sin is a crime. Thus we can say of the life of holy men even while they live in this mortality, that they are found without crime. *"If we say that we have no sin,"* as the great apostle says, *"we deceive ourselves, and the truth is not in us."*[141]

65. Nevertheless, no matter how great our crimes, their forgiveness should never be despaired of in holy church for those who truly repent, each according to the measure of his sin. And, in the act of repentance,[142] where a crime has been committed of such gravity as also to cut off the sinner from the body of Christ, we should not consider the measure of time as much as the measure of sorrow. For, *"a broken and a contrite heart, O God, thou wilt not despise."*[143]

Still, since the sorrow of one heart is mostly hid from another, and does not come to notice through words and other such signs—even when it is plain to Him of whom it is said, *"My groaning is not hid from thee"*[144]—times of repentance have been rightly established by those set over

141. 1 John 1:8.
142. In *actione poenitentiae*; see Luther's similar conception of *poenitentiam agite* in the 95 *Theses* and in *De poenitentia*.
143. Psalm 51:17.
144. Psalm 38:9.

the churches, that satisfaction may also be made in the church, in which the sins are forgiven. For, of course, outside her they are not forgiven. For she alone has received the pledge of the Holy Spirit,[145] without whom there is no forgiveness of sins. Those forgiven thus obtain life everlasting.

66. Now the remission of sins has chiefly to do with the future judgment. In this life the Scripture saying holds true: "A heavy yoke is on the sons of Adam, from the day they come forth from their mother's womb till the day of their burial in the mother of us all."[146] Thus we see even infants, after the washing of regeneration, tortured by divers evil afflictions. This helps us to understand that the whole import of the sacraments of salvation has to do more with the hope of future goods than with the retaining or attaining of present goods.

Indeed, many sins seem to be ignored and go unpunished; but their punishment is reserved for the future. It is not in vain that the day when the Judge of the living and the dead shall come is rightly called the day of judgment. Just so, on the other hand, some sins are punished here, and, if they are forgiven, will certainly bring no harm upon us in the future age. Hence, referring to certain temporal punishments, which are visited upon sinners in this life, the apostle, speaking to those whose sins are blotted out and not reserved to the end, says: *"For if we would judge*

145. See 2 Corinthians 1:22.
146. Ecclesiasticusus 40:1 (Vulgate).

ourselves, we should not be judged. But when we are judged, we are chastened of the Lord, that we should not be condemned with the world."[147]

147. 1 Corinthians 11:31–32.

18

Faith and Works[148]

67. There are some, indeed, who believe that those who do not abandon the name of Christ, and who are baptized in His laver in the church, who are not cut off from it by schism or heresy, who may then live in sins however great, not washing them away by repentance, nor redeeming them by alms—and who obstinately persevere in them to life's last day—even these will still be saved, "though as by fire." They believe that such people will be punished by fire, prolonged in proportion to their sins, but still not eternal.

But those who believe thus, and still are Catholics, are deceived, as it seems to me, by a kind of merely human benevolence. For the divine Scripture, when consulted, answers differently. Moreover, I have written a book about

148. This chapter supplies an important clue to the date of the Enchiridion and an interesting side light on Augustine's inclination to re-use "good material." In his treatise on The Eight Questions of Dulcitius (*De Octo Dulcitii Quaestionibus*), 1:10–13, Augustine quotes this entire chapter as a part of his answer to the question whether those who sin after baptism are ever delivered from hell. The date of the *De Octo* is 422 or, possibly, 423; thus we have a *terminus ad quem* for the date of the Enchiridion. Still the best text of *De Octo* is Migne, PL, 40, c. 147–170, and the best English translation is in *Deferrari*, St. Augustine: *Treatises on Various Subjects* (The Fathers of the Church, New York, 1952), pp. 427–466.

this question, entitled faith and works,[149] in which, with God's help, I have shown as best I could that, according to Holy Scripture, the faith that saves is the faith that the apostle Paul adequately describes when he says, *"For in Jesus Christ neither circumcision availeth any thing, nor uncircumcision; but the faith which worketh by love."*[150] But if faith works evil and not good, then without doubt, according to the apostle James *"is dead, being alone."*[151] He then goes on to say, *"Though a man say he hath faith, and hath not works? can faith save him?"*[152]

Now, if the wicked man were to be saved by fire on account of his faith only, and if this is the way the statement of the blessed Paul should be understood—*"But he himself shall be saved; yet so as by fire"*[153]—then faith without works would be sufficient to salvation. But then what the apostle James said would be false. And also false would be another statement of the same Paul himself: *"Be not deceived,"* he says, *"neither fornicators, nor idolaters, nor adulterers, nor effeminate, nor abusers of themselves with mankind, nor thieves, nor covetous, nor drunkards, nor revilers,*

149. A short treatise, written in 413, in which Augustine seeks to combine the Pauline and Jacobite emphases by analyzing what kind of faith and what kind of works are both essential to salvation. The best text is that of Joseph Zycha in CSEL, Vol. 41, and pp. 35-97; but see also *Migne*, PL, 40, c. 197-230. There is an English translation by C.L. Cornish in A Library of Fathers of the Holy Catholic Church; *Seventeen Short Treatises*, pp. 37–84.
150. Galatians 5:6.
151. James 2:17.
152. Verse 14.
153. 1 Corinthians 3:15

nor extortioners, shall inherit the kingdom of God."[154] Now, if those who persist in such crimes as these are nevertheless saved by their faith in Christ, would they not then be in the kingdom of God?

68. But, since these fully plain and most pertinent apostolic testimonies cannot be false, that one obscure saying about those who build on *"the foundation* [which is Christ, not] *gold, silver, precious stones, wood, hay, and stubble"*[155]—for it is about these it is said that they will be saved as by fire, not perishing on account of the saving worth of their foundation—such a statement must be interpreted so that it does not contradict these fully plain testimonies.

In fact, wood and hay and stubble may be understood, without absurdity, to signify such an attachment to those worldly things—albeit legitimate in themselves—that one cannot suffer their loss without anguish in the soul. Now, when such anguish "burns," and Christ still holds His place as foundation in the heart—that is, if nothing is preferred to Him and if the man whose anguish "burns" would still prefer to suffer loss of the things he greatly loves than to lose Christ—then one is saved, "by fire." But if, in time of testing, he should prefer to hold onto these temporal and worldly goods rather than to Christ, he does not have Him as foundation—because he has put "things"

154. 1 Corinthians 6:9–10
155. 1 Corinthians 3:12

in the first place—whereas in a building nothing comes before the foundations.

Now, this fire, of which the apostle speaks, should be understood as one through which both kinds of men must pass: that is, the man who builds with gold, silver, and precious stones on this foundation and also the man who builds with wood, hay, and stubble. For, when he had spoken of this, he added: "*The fire shall try every man's work of what sort it is. If any man's work abide which he has built thereupon, he shall receive a reward. If any man's work shall be burned, he shall suffer loss: but he himself shall be saved; yet so as by fire.*"[156] Therefore the fire will test the work, not only of the one, but of both.

The fire is a sort of trial of affliction, concerning which it is clearly written elsewhere: "The furnace proveth the potter's vessels, so the trial of man is in his reasoning."[157] This kind of fireworks in the span of this life, just as the apostle said, as it affects the two different kinds of faithful men. There is, for example, the man who "thinks of the things of God, how he may please God." Such a man builds on Christ the foundation, with gold, silver, and precious stones. The other man "*careth for the things that are of the world, how he may please his wife*"[158]; that is, he builds upon the same foundation with wood, hay, and stubble. The work of the former

156. 1 Corinthians 3:13-15.
157. Ecclesiasticus 27:5 (Apocrypha).
158. 1 Corinthians 7:33.

is not burned up, since he has not loved those things whose loss brings anguish. But the work of the latter is burned up, since things are not lost without anguish when they have been loved with a possessive love. But because, in this second situation, he prefers to suffer the loss of these things rather than losing Christ, and does not desert Christ from fear of losing such things—even though he may grieve over his loss—"he is saved," indeed, "yet so as by fire." He "burns" with grief, for the things he has loved and lost, but this does not subvert nor consume him, secured as he is by the stability and the indestructibility of his foundation.

69. It is not incredible that something like this should occur after this life, whether or not it is a matter for fruitful inquiry. It may be discovered or remain hidden whether some of the faithful are sooner or later to be saved by a sort of purgatorial fire, in proportion as they have loved the goods that perish, and in proportion to their attachment to them. However, this does not apply to those of whom it was said, they *"shall* [not] *inherit the kingdom of God,"*[159] unless their crimes are remitted through due repentance. I say "due repentance" to signify that they must not be barren of almsgiving, on which divine Scripture lays so much stress that our Lord tells us in advance that, on the bare basis of fruitfulness in alms, He will impute merit to those on His right hand; and, on the same basis of unfruitfulness,

159. 1 Corinthians 6:10.

demerit to those on His left—when He shall say to the former, *"Come, ye blessed of my Father, inherit the kingdom,"* but to the latter, *"Depart…into everlasting fire."*[160]

160. Matthew 25:34, 41.

19

Almsgiving and Forgiveness

70. We must beware, however, lest anyone suppose that unspeakable crimes such as they commit who *"will not inherit the kingdom of God"* can be perpetrated daily and then daily redeemed by almsgiving. Of course, life must be changed for the better, and alms should be offered as propitiation to God for our past sins. But he is not somehow to be bought off, as if we always had a license to commit crimes with impunity. For, "neither hath he has given any man license to sin"[161]—although, in His mercy, He does blot out sins already committed, if due satisfaction for them is not neglected.

71. For the passing and trivial sins of every day, from which no life is free, the everyday prayer of the faithful makes satisfaction. For they can say, *"Our Father which art in heaven,"*[162] who have already been reborn to such a Father *"of water and of the Spirit."*[163] This prayer completely blots out our minor and everyday sins. It also blots out those sins which once made the life of the faithful wicked, but from which, now that they have changed for the better by repentance, they

161. Ecclesiasticus 15:20 (Apocrypha).

162. Matthew 6:9.

163. John 3:5.

have departed. The condition of this is that just as they truly say, *"Forgive us our debts"* (since there is no lack of debts to be forgiven), so also they truly say, *"As we forgive our debtors"*[164]; that is, if what is said is also done. For to forgive a man who seeks forgiveness is indeed to give alms.

72. Accordingly, what our Lord says—*"Give alms… and, behold, all things are clean unto you"*[165]—applies to all useful acts of mercy. Therefore, not only the man who gives food to the hungry, drink to the thirsty, clothing to the naked, hospitality to the wayfarer, refuge to the fugitive; who visits the sick and the prisoner, redeems the captive, bears the burdens of the weak, leads the blind, comforts the sorrowful, heals the sick, shows the errant the right way, gives advice to the perplexed, and does whatever is needful for the needy[166]—not only does this man give alms, but the man who forgives the trespasser also gives alms as well. He is also a giver of alms who, by blows or other discipline, corrects and restrains those under his command, if at the same time he forgives from the heart the sin by which he has been wronged or offended, or prays that it be forgiven the offender. Such a man gives alms, not only in that he forgives and prays, but also in that he

164. Matthew 6:12.

165. Luke 11:41.

166. This is a close approximation of the medieval lists of "The Seven Works of Mercy." See J.T. McNeill, *A History of the Cure of Souls*, pp. 155, 161. (Harper & Brothers, 1951, New York.)

rebukes and administers corrective punishment, since in this he shows mercy.

Now, many benefits are bestowed on the unwilling, when their interests and not their preferences are consulted. And men frequently are found to be their own enemies, while those they suppose to be their enemies are their true friends. And then, by mistake, they return evil for good, when a Christian ought not to return evil even for evil. Thus, there are many kinds of alms, by which, when we do them, we are helped in obtaining forgiveness of our own sins.

73. But none of these alms is greater than the forgiveness from the heart of a sin committed against us by someone else. It is a smaller thing to wish well or even to do well to one who has done you no evil. It is far greater—a sort of magnificent goodness—to love your enemy, and always to wish him well and, as you can, do well to him who wishes you ill and who does you harm when he can. Thus one heeds God's command: *"Love your enemies, bless them that curse you,...and pray for them which...persecute you."*[167]

Such counsels are for the perfect sons of God. And although all the faithful should strive toward them and through prayer to God and earnest endeavor bring their souls up to this level, still so high a degree of goodness is not possible for so great a multitude as we believe are

167. Matthew 5:44.

heard when, in prayer, they say, "Forgive us our debts, as we forgive our debtors." Accordingly, it cannot be doubted that the terms of this pledge are fulfilled if a man, not yet so perfect that he already loves his enemies, still forgives from the heart one who has sinned against him and who now asks his forgiveness. For he surely seeks forgiveness when he asks for it when he prays, saying, "As we forgive our debtors." For this means, "Forgive us our debts when we ask for forgiveness, as we also forgive our debtors when they ask for forgiveness."

74. Again, if one seeks forgiveness from a man against whom he sinned—moved by his sin to seek it—he should no longer be regarded as an enemy, and it should not now be as difficult to love him as it was when he was actively hostile. Now, a man who does not forgive from the heart one who asks forgiveness and is repentant of his sins can in no way suppose that his own sins are forgiven by the Lord, since the truth cannot lie, and what hearer and reader of the gospel has not noted who it was who said, *"I am… the truth"*[168]? It is, of course, the One who, when He was teaching the prayer, strongly emphasized this sentence which He put in it, saying: *"For if ye forgive men their trespasses, your heavenly Father will also forgive you: but if ye forgive not men their trespasses, neither will your Father forgive your trespasses."*[169] He who is not

168. John 14:6.
169. Matthew 6:14–15.

awakened by such great thundering is not asleep, but dead. And yet such a word has power to awaken even the dead.

20

Spiritual Almsgiving

75. Now, surely, those who live in gross wickedness and take no care to correct their lives and habits, who yet, amid their crimes and misdeeds, continue to multiply their alms, flatter themselves in vain with the Lord's words, "*Give alms…and, behold, all things are clean unto you.*" They do not understand how far this saying reaches. In order for them to understand, let them notice to whom it was that he said it. For this is the context of it in the gospel:

> *As he spake, a certain Pharisee besought him to dine with him: and he went in, and sat down to meat. And when the Pharisee saw it, he marveled that he had not first washed before dinner. And the Lord said unto him, Now do ye Pharisees make clean the outside of the cup and the platter; but your inward part is full of ravening and wickedness. Ye fools, did not he that made that which is without make that which is within also? But rather give alms of such things as ye have; and, behold, all things are clean unto you.*[170]

170. Luke 11:37–41.

Should we interpret this to mean that to the Pharisees, who had not the faith of Christ, all things are clean if only they give alms, as they deem it right to give them, even if they have not believed in Him, nor been reborn of water and the Spirit? But all are unclean who are not made clean by the faith of Christ, of whom it is written, *"Purifying their hearts by faith."*[171] And as the apostle said, *"But unto them that are defiled and unbelieving is nothing pure; both even their mind and conscience is defiled."*[172] How, then, should all things be clean to the Pharisees, even if they gave alms, but were not believers? Or, how could they be believers, if they were unwilling to believe in Christ and to be born again in His grace? And yet, what they heard is true: *"Give alms…and behold, all things are clean unto you."*

76. He who would give alms as a set plan of his life should begin with himself and give them to himself. For almsgiving is a work of mercy, and the saying is most true: "Have mercy upon your own soul, pleasing God."[173] The purpose of the new birth is that we should become pleasing to God, who is justly displeased with the sin we contracted in birth. This is the first almsgiving, which we give to ourselves—when through the mercy of a merciful God we come to inquire about our wretchedness and come to acknowledge the just verdict by which we were put in need of that mercy, of which the apostle says, *"Judgment came*

171. Acts 15:9.

172. Titus 1:15.

173. Ecclesiasticus 30:24 (Vulgate).

upon all men to condemnation."[174] And the same herald of grace then adds (in a word of thanksgiving for God's great love), *"But God commendeth his love toward us, in that, while we were yet sinners, Christ died for us."*[175] Thus, when we come to a valid estimate of our wretchedness and begin to love God with the love He Himself giveth us, we then begin to live piously and righteously.

But the Pharisees, while they gave as alms a tithing of even the least of their fruits, disregarded this "judgment and love of God." Therefore, they did not begin their almsgiving with themselves, nor did they, first of all, show mercy toward themselves. In reference to this right order of self-love, it was said, *"Thou shalt love thy neighbor as thyself."*[176]

Therefore, when the Lord had reproved the Pharisees for washing themselves on the outside while inwardly they were still full of extortion and wickedness, He then admonished them also to give those alms that a man owes first to himself—to make clean the inner man: *"But rather,"* He said, *"give alms of such things as ye have, and, behold, all things are clean unto you."* Then, to make plain the import of His admonition, which they had ignored, and to show them that He was not ignorant of their kind of almsgiving, He adds, *"But woe unto you, Pharisees!"*[177]—as if to say, "I am advising you to give the kind of alms

174. Romans 5:18.
175. Romans 5:8.
176. Mark 12:31.
177. Luke 11:42

which shall make all things clean to you." "But woe to you, for you tithe mint and rue and every herb"—"I know these alms of yours and you need not think I am admonishing you to give them up"—"and then neglect justice and the love of God." "This kind of almsgiving would make you clean from all inward defilement, just as the bodies which you wash are made clean by you." For the word "all" here means both "inward" and "outward"—as elsewhere we read, *"Cleanse first that which is within the cup and platter, that the outside of them may become clean also."*[178] But, lest it appear that He was rejecting the kind of alms we give of the earth's bounty, He adds, *"These ought ye to have done"*—that is, pay heed to the judgment and love of God—and *"not to leave the other undone"*[179]—that is, alms done with the earth's bounty.

77. Therefore, let them not deceive themselves who suppose that by giving alms—however profusely, and whether of their fruits or money or anything else—they purchase impunity to continue in the enormity of their crimes and the grossness of their wickedness. For not only do they do such things, but they also love them so much that they would always choose to continue in them—if they could do so with impunity. "But he who loves iniquity hates his own soul."[180] And he who hates his own soul is not merciful but cruel to it. For by loving it after the world's way he hates it according to God's way of judging.

178. Matthew 23:26.

179. Verse 23.

180. Psalm 10:6 (Vulgate).

Therefore, if one really wished to give alms to himself, that all things might become clean to him, he would hate his soul after the world's way and love it according to God's way. No one, however, gives any alms at all unless he gives from the store of Him who needs not anything. "Accordingly," it is said, "His mercy shall go before me."[181]

181. Psalm 58:11 (Vulgate); see also Psalm 59:10 RSV.

21

Problems of Casuistry

78. What sins are trivial and what are grave, however, is not for human but for divine judgment to determine. For we see that, in respect of some sins, even the apostle, by pardoning them, has conceded this point. Such a case is seen in what the venerable Paul says to married folks: *"Defraud ye not one the other, except it be with consent for a time, that ye may give yourselves to fasting and prayer; and come together again, that Satan tempt you not for your incontinency."*[182] One could consider that it is not a sin for a married couple to have intercourse, not only for the sake of procreating children—which is the good of marriage—but also for the sake of the carnal pleasure involved. Thus, those whose self-control is weak could avoid fornication, or adultery, and other kinds of impurity too shameful to name, into which their lust might drag them through Satan's tempting. Therefore one could, as I said, consider this not a sin, had the apostle not added, *"But I speak this by permission, and not of commandment."*[183] Who, then, denies that it is a sin when he agrees that apostolic authority for doing it is given only by *"concession"*?

182. 1 Corinthians 7:5.

183. Verse 6.

Another such case is seen where he says, *"Dare any of you, having a matter against another, go to law before the unjust, and not before the saints?"*[184] And a bit later:

> *If then ye have judgments of things pertaining to this life, set them to judge who are least esteemed in the church. I speak to your shame. Is it so, that there is not a wise man among you? No, not one that shall be able to judge between his brethren? But brother goeth to law with brother, and that before the unbelievers.*[185]

And here it might be thought that it was not a sin to bring suit against a brother, and that the only sin consisted in wishing it judged outside the church, if the apostle had not added immediately, *"Now therefore there is utterly a fault among you, because ye go to law one with another."*[186] Then, lest someone excuse himself on this point by saying that he had a just cause and was suffering injustice that he wished removed by judicial sentence, the apostle directly resists such thoughts and excuses by saying: *"Why do ye not rather suffer yourselves to be defrauded?"*[187] Thus we are brought back to that saying of the Lord: *"If any man would sue thee at law and take thy coat, let him have thy cloak also."*[188] And in another place: *"And of him that taketh away*

184. 1 Corinthians 6:1.
185. Verses 4–6.
186. Verse 7.
187. Verse 7.
188. Matthew 5:40.

thy goods ask them not again."[189] Thus, he forbids his own to go to court with other men in secular suits. And it is because of this teaching that the apostle says that this kind of action is "a fault." Still, when he allows such suits to be decided in the church, brothers judging brothers, yet sternly forbids such a thing outside the church, it is clear that some concession is being made here for the infirmities of the weak.

Because of these and similar sins—and of others even less than these, such as offenses in words and thoughts—and because, as the apostle James confesses, "*in many things we offend all,*"[190] it behooves us to pray to the Lord daily and often, and say, "Forgive us our debts," and not lie about what follows this petition, "As we also forgive our debtors."

79. There are, however, some sins that could be deemed quite trifling if the Scriptures did not show that they are more serious than we think. For who would suppose that one saying to his brother, "You fool," is "in danger of hell-fire," if the Truth had not said it? Still, for the hurt he immediately supplied a medicine, adding the precept of brotherly reconciliation: "*Therefore if thou bring thy gift to the altar, and there rememberest that thy brother hath ought against thee,*"[191] etc.

189. Luke 6:30.
190. James 3:2.
191. Matthew 5:23.

Or who would think how great a sin it is to observe days and months and years and seasons—as those people do who will or will not begin projects on certain days or in certain months or years, because they follow vain human doctrines and suppose that various seasons are lucky or unlucky—if we did not infer the magnitude of this evil from the apostle's fear, in saying to such men, *"I am afraid of you, lest I have bestowed upon you labor in vain"*[192]?

80. To this one might add those sins, however grave and terrible, which, when they come to be habitual, are then believed to be trivial or no sins at all. And so far does this go that such sins are not only not kept secret, but are even proclaimed and published abroad—cases of which it is written, "The sinner is praised in the desires of his soul; and he that works iniquity is blessed."[193]

In the divine books such iniquity is called a "cry" (clamor). You have such a usage in the prophet Isaiah's reference to the evil vineyard: "[I] *looked for justice, but behold, bloodshed; for righteousness, but behold, a cry."*[194] So also is that passage in Genesis: *"The cry of Sodom and Gomorrah is great,"*[195] for among these people such crimes were not only unpunished, but were openly committed, as if sanctioned by law.

192. Galatians 4:11.
193. Psalm 10:3 (Vulgate).
194. Isaiah 5:7 RSVCE.
195. Genesis 18:20.

So also in our times so many evils, even if not like those (of old), have come to be public customs that we not only do not dare excommunicate a layman; we do not dare degrade a clergyman for them. Thus, several years ago, when I was expounding the Epistle to the Galatians, where the apostle says, *"I am afraid of you, lest I have bestowed upon you labor in vain,"* I was moved to exclaim: "Woe to the sins of men! We shrink from them only when we are not accustomed to them. As for those sins to which we are accustomed—although the blood of the Son of God was shed to wash them away—although they are so great that the kingdom of God is wholly closed to them, yet, living with them often we come to tolerate them, and, tolerating them, we even practice some of them! But grant, O Lord, that we do not practice any of them which we could prohibit!" I shall someday know whether immoderate indignation moved me here to speak rashly.

22

The Two Causes of Sin

81. I shall now mention what I have often discussed before in other places in my short treatises.[196] We sin from two causes: either from not seeing what we ought to do, or else from not doing what we have already seen we ought to do. Of these two, the first is ignorance of the evil; the second, weakness.

We must surely fight against both; but we shall as surely be defeated unless we are divinely helped, not only to see what we ought to do, but also, as sound judgment increases, to make our love of righteousness victor over our love of those things because of which—either by desiring to possess them or by fearing to lose them—we fall, open-eyed, into known sin. In this latter case, we are not only sinners—which we are even when we sin through ignorance—but also lawbreakers: for we do not do what we should, and we do what we know already we should not.

Accordingly, we should pray for pardon if we have sinned, as we do when we say, "Forgive us our debts as

---

196. For example, *Contra Faustum*, Book 22:78; *De Peccatorum Meritis et Remissione*, I, 39:70; ibid., II, 22:26; *Quaestiones in Heptateuch*, 4:24; *De Libero Arbitrio*, 3:18, 55; *De Diversis Quaestioninbus*, 83:26; *De Natura et Gratia*, 67:81; *Contra Duas Epistulas. Pelagianorum*, 1:3, 7; 1:13:27.

we also forgive our debtors." But we should also pray that God should guide us away from sin, and this we do when we say, "Lead us not into temptation"—and we should make our petitions to Him of whom it is said in the psalm, *"The LORD is my light and my salvation"*[197]; that, as light, He may take away our ignorance, as salvation, our weakness.

82. Now, penance itself is often omitted because of weakness, even when in church custom there is an adequate reason why it should be performed. For shame is the fear of displeasing men, when a man loves their good opinion more than he regards judgment, which would make him humble himself in penitence. Wherefore, not only for one to repent, but also in order that he may be enabled to do so, the mercy of God is prerequisite. Otherwise, the apostle would not say of some men, *in case "God…will give them repentance."*[198] And, similarly, that Peter might be enabled to weep bitterly, the evangelist tells, *"The LORD looked upon him."*[199]

83. But the man who does not believe that sins are forgiven in the church, who despises so great a bounty of the divine gifts and ends, and persists to his last day in such an obstinacy of mind—that man is guilty of the unpardonable sin against the Holy Spirit, in whom Christ forgives

197. Psalm 27:1.
198. 2 Timothy 2:25.
199. Judges 6:14.

sins.[200] I have discussed this difficult question, as clearly as I could, in a little book devoted exclusively to this very point.[201]

---

200. See John 20:22–23.
201. This libellus is included in Augustine's Sermons (LXXI, PL, 38, col. 445–467), to which Possidius gave the title *De Blasphemia in Spiritum Sanctum*. English translation in N-PNF, 1st Series, Vol. VI, Sermon XXI, pp. 318–332.

23

The Reality of the Resurrection

84. Now, with respect to the resurrection of the body—and by this I do not mean the cases of resuscitation after which people died again, but a resurrection to eternal life after the fashion of Christ's own body—I have not found a way to discuss it briefly and still give satisfactory answers to all the questions usually raised about it. Yet no Christian should have the slightest doubt as to the fact that the bodies of all men, whether already or yet to be born, whether dead or still to die, will be resurrected.

85. Once this fact is established, then, first of all, comes the question about abortive fetuses, which are indeed "born" in the mother's womb, but are never so that they could be "reborn." For, if we say that there is a resurrection for them, then we can agree that at least as much is true of fetuses that are fully formed. But, with regard to undeveloped fetuses, who would not more readily think that they perish, like seeds that did not germinate?[202]

But who, then, would dare to deny—though he would not dare to affirm it either—that in the resurrection day

202. *Sicut semina quae concepta non fuerint.*

what is lacking in the forms of things will be filled out? Thus, the perfection that time would have accomplished will not be lacking, any more than the blemishes wrought by time will still be present. Nature, then, will be cheated of nothing apt and fitting that time's passage would have brought, nor will anything remain disfigured by anything adverse and contrary that time has wrought. But what is not yet a whole will become whole, just as what has been disfigured will be restored to its full figure.

86. On this score, a corollary question may be most carefully discussed by the most learned men, and still I do not know that any man can answer it, namely: When does a human being begin to live in the womb? Is there some form of hidden life, not yet apparent in the motions of a living thing? To deny, for example, that those fetuses ever lived at all that are cut away limb by limb and cast out of the wombs of pregnant women, lest the mothers die also if the fetuses were left there dead, would seem much too rash. But, in any case, once a man begins to live, it is thereafter possible for him to die. And, once dead, wheresoever death overtook him, I cannot find the basis on which he would not have a share in the resurrection of the dead.

87. By the same token, the resurrection is not to be denied in the cases of monsters that are born and live, even if they quickly die, nor should we believe that they will be raised as they were, but rather in an amended nature and free from faults. Far be it from us to say of

that double-limbed man recently born in the Orient—about whom most reliable brethren have given eyewitness reports and the presbyter Jerome, of holy memory, has left a written account[203]—far be it from us, I say, to suppose that at the resurrection there will be one double man, and not rather two men, as there would have been if they had actually been born twins. So also in other cases, which, because of some excess or defect or gross deformity, are called monsters: at the resurrection they will be restored to the normal human physiognomy, so that every soul will have its own body and not two bodies joined together, even though they were born this way. Every soul will have, as its own, all that is required to complete a whole human body.

88. Moreover, with God, the earthly substance from which the flesh of mortal man is produced does not perish. Instead, whether it be dissolved into dust or ashes, or dispersed into vapors and the winds, or converted into the substance of other bodies (or even back into the basic elements themselves), or has served as food for beasts or even men and been turned into their flesh—in an instant of time this matter returns to the soul that first animated it, and that caused it to become a man, to live and to grow.

89. This earthly matter that becomes a corpse upon the soul's departure will not, at the resurrection, be so

203. Jerome, *Epistle to Vitalis,* Ep. LXXII, 2; PL, 22, 674. Augustine also refers to similar phenomena in *The City of God,* XVI. viii, 2.

restored that the parts into which it was separated and which have become parts of other things must necessarily return to the same parts of the body in which they were situated—though they do return to the body from which they were separated. Otherwise, to suppose that the hair recovers what frequent clippings have taken off, or the nails get back what trimming has pared off, makes for a wild and wholly unbecoming image in the minds of those who speculate this way and leads them thus to disbelieve in the resurrection. But take the example of a statue made of fusible metal: if it were melted by heat or pounded into dust, or reduced to a shapeless mass, and an artist wished to restore it again from the mass of the same material, it would make no difference to the wholeness of the restored statue which part of it was remade of what part of the metal, so long as the statue, as restored, had been given all the material of which it was originally composed. Just so, God—an artist who works in marvelous and mysterious ways—will restore our bodies, with marvelous and mysterious celerity, out of the whole of the matter of which it was originally composed. And it will make no difference, in the restoration, whether hair returns to hair and nails to nails, or whether the part of this original matter that had perished is turned back into flesh and restored to other parts of the body. The main thing is that the providence of the (divine) Artist takes care that nothing unbecoming will result.

90. Nor does it follow that the stature of each person will be different when brought to life anew because there were differences in stature when first alive, nor that the lean will be raised lean or the fat come back to life in their former obesity. But if this is in the Creator's plan, that each shall retain his special features and the proper and recognizable likeness of his former self—while an equality of physical endowment will be preserved—then the matter of which each resurrection body is composed will be so disposed that none shall be lost, and any defect will be supplied by Him who can create out of nothing as he wills.

But if in the bodies of those rising again there is to be an intelligible inequality, such as between voices that fill out a chorus, this will be managed by disposing the matter of each body so to bring men into their place in the angelic band and impose nothing on their senses that is inharmonious. For surely nothing unseemly will be there, and whatever is there will be fitting, and this because the unfitting will simply not be.

91. The bodies of the saints, then, shall rise again free from blemish and deformity, just as they will be also free from corruption, encumbrance, or handicap. Their facility (*facilitas*) will be as complete as their felicity (*Felicitas*). This is why their bodies are called "spiritual," though undoubtedly they will be bodies and not spirits. For just as now the body is called "animate" (*animale*), though it is

a body and not a "spirit" (*anima*), so then it will be a "spiritual body," but still a body and not a spirit.

Accordingly, then, as far as the corruption that weighs down the soul and the vices through which "*the flesh lusteth against the Spirit*"[204] are concerned, there will be no "flesh," but only body, since there are bodies that are called "*celestial bodies.*"[205] This is why it is said, "*flesh and blood cannot inherit the kingdom of God,*" and then, as if to expound what was said, it adds, "*Neither doth corruption inherit incorruption.*"[206] What the writer first called "*flesh and blood*" he later called "*corruption,*" and what he first called "*the kingdom of God*" he then later called "*incorruption.*"[207]

But, as far as the substance of the resurrection body is concerned, it will even then still be "flesh." This is why the body of Christ is called "flesh" even after the resurrection. Wherefore the apostle also says, "[What] *is sown a natural body [corpus animale]; it is raised a spiritual body [corpus spiritual].*"[208] For there will then be such a concord between flesh and spirit—the spirit quickening the servant flesh without any need of sustenance therefrom—that there will be no further conflict within ourselves. And just as there will be no more external enemies to bear

---

204 Galatians 5:17.
205. 1 Corinthians 15:40.
206. Verse 50.
207. Ibid.
208. Verse 44.

with, so neither shall we have to bear with ourselves as enemies within.

92. But whoever are not liberated from that mass of perdition (brought to pass through the first man) by the one Mediator between God and man, they will also rise again, each in his own flesh, but only that they may be punished together with the devil and his angels. Whether these men will rise again with all their faults and deformities, with their diseased and deformed members—is there any reason for us to labor such a question? For obviously the uncertainty about their bodily form and beauty need not weary us, since their damnation is certain and eternal.

And let us not be moved to inquire how their body can be incorruptible if it can suffer—or corruptible if it cannot die. For there is no true life unless it be lived in happiness; no true incorruptibility save where health is unscathed by pain. But where an unhappy being is not allowed to die, then death itself, so to say, dies not; and where pain perpetually afflicts but never destroys, corruption goes on endlessly. This state is called, in the Scripture, *"the second death."*[209]

93. Yet neither the first death, in which the soul is compelled to leave its body, nor the second death, in which it is not allowed to leave the body undergoing punishment, would have befallen man if no one had sinned. Surely, the

---

209. Revelation 2:11; 20:6, 14.

lightest of all punishments will be laid on those who have added no further sin to that originally contracted. Among the rest, who have added further sins to that one, they will suffer a damnation somewhat more tolerable in proportion to the lesser degree of their iniquity.

24

The Solution to Present Spiritual Enigmas to Be Awaited in the Life of the World To Come

94. And thus it will be that while the reprobated angels and men go on in their eternal punishment, the saints will go on learning more fully the blessings that grace has bestowed upon them. Then, through the actual realities of their experience, they will see more clearly the meaning of what is written in Psalms: *"I will sing of mercy and judgment: unto thee, O Lord"*[210]—since no one is set free save by unmerited mercy and no one is damned save by a merited condemnation.

95. Then what is now hidden will not be hidden: when one of two infants is taken up by God's mercy and the other abandoned through God's judgment—and when the chosen one knows what would have been his just deserts in judgment—why was the one chosen rather than the other, when the condition of the two was the same? Or again, why were miracles not wrought in the presence of certain people who would have repented in the face of miraculous works, while miracles were wrought in the presence of those who were not about to believe. For our Lord says most plainly: *"Woe to thee,*

210. Psalm 101:1.

Chorazin! woe to thee, Bethsaida! for if the mighty works, which were done in you, had been done in Tyre and Sidon, they would have repented long ago in sackcloth and ashes."[211] Now, obviously, God did not act unjustly in not willing their salvation, even though they could have been saved, if he willed it so.[212]

Then, in the clearest light of wisdom, will be seen what now the pious hold by faith, not yet grasping it in clear understanding—how certain, immutable, and effectual is the will of God, how there are things He can do but does not will to do, yet wills nothing He cannot do, and how true is what is sung in the psalm: "But our God is above in heaven; in heaven and on earth he hath done all things whatsoever that he would."[213] This obviously is

211. Matthew 11:21.

212. This is one of the rare instances in which a textual variant in Augustine's text affects a basic issue in the interpretation of his doctrine. All but one of the major old editions, up to and including *Migne*, here read: Nec utique deus injuste noluit salvos fiere eum possent salvi esse *si vellent* (if they willed it). This would mean the attribution of a decisive role in human salvation to the human will and would thus stand out in bold relief from his general stress in the rest of the *Enchiridion* and elsewhere on the primacy and even irresistibility of grace. The Jansenist edition of Augustine, by Arnauld in 1648, read *si vellet* (if He willed it) and the reading became the subject of acrimonious controversy between the Jansenists and the Molinists. The Maurist edition reads *si vellet*, on the strength of much additional MS. evidence that had not been available up to that time. In modern times, the *si vellet* reading has come to have the overwhelming support of the critical editors, although Rivière still reads *si vellent*. See Scheel, 76–77 (See Bibl.); Rivière, 402–403; J. G. Krabinger, S. Aurelii Augustini Enchiridion (Tübingen, 1861), p. 116; Faure-Passaglia, S. Aurelii Augustini Enchiridion (Naples, 1847), p. 178; and H. Hurter, Sanctorum Patrum opuscula selecta (Innsbruck, 1895), p. 123.

213. See Psalm 113:11 (a mixed text; composed inexactly from Psalm 115:3 and Psalm 135:6; an interesting instance of Augustine's sense of liberty with the texts of Scripture. Here he is doubtless quoting from memory).

not true, if there is anything that He willed to do and did not do, or, what were worse, if He did not do something because man's will prevented Him, the Omnipotent, from doing what He willed. Nothing, therefore, happens unless the Omnipotent wills it to happen. He either allows it to happen or He actually causes it to happen.

96. Nor should we doubt that God does well, even when He allows whatever happens ill to happen. For He allows it only through a just judgment—and surely all that is just is good. Therefore, although evil, in so far as it is evil, is not good, still it is a good thing that not only good things exist but evil as well. For if it were not good that evil things exist, they would certainly not be allowed to exist by the Omnipotent Good, for whom it is undoubtedly as easy not to allow to exist what He does not will, as it is for Him to do what He does will.

Unless we believe this, the very beginning of our confession of faith is imperiled—the sentence in which we profess to believe in God the Father Almighty. For He is called almighty for no other reason than that He can do whatsoever He wills and because the efficacy of His omnipotent will is not impeded by the will of any creature.

97. Accordingly, we must now inquire about the meaning of what was said most truly by the apostle concerning God, "*Who will have all men to be saved.*"[214] For

---

214. 1 Timothy 2:4.

since not all—not even a majority—are saved, it would indeed appear that the fact that what God wills to happen does not happen is due to an embargo on God's will by the human will.

Now, when we ask for the reason why not all are saved, the customary answer is: "Because they themselves have not willed it." But this cannot be said of infants, who have not yet come to the power of willing or not willing. For, if we could attribute to their wills the infant squirmings they make at baptism, when they resist as hard as they can, we would then have to say that they were saved against their will. But the Lord's language is clearer when, in the gospel, He reproves the unrighteous city: *"How often,"* He says, *"would I have gathered thy children together, even as a hen gathereth her chickens under her wings, and ye would not!"*[215] This sounds as if God's will had been overcome by human wills and as if the weakest, by not willing, impeded the Most Powerful so that He could not do what He willed. And where is that omnipotence by which "whatsoever He willed in heaven and on earth, He has done," if He willed to gather the children of Jerusalem together, and did not do so? Or, is it not rather the case that, although Jerusalem did not will that her children be gathered together by Him, yet, despite her unwillingness, God did indeed gather together those children of hers whom He would? It is not that "in heaven and on earth" He has

215. Matthew 23:37.

willed and done some things, and willed other things and not done them. Instead, "all things whatsoever He willed, He hath done."

25

Predestination and the Justice of God

98. Furthermore, who would be so impiously foolish as to say that God cannot turn the evil wills of men—as He wills, when He wills, and where He wills—toward the good? But, when He acts, He acts through mercy; when He does not act, it is through justice. For, "*hath he mercy on whom he will hath mercy, and whom he will he hardeneth.*"[216]

Now when the apostle said this, he was commending grace, of which he had just spoken in connection with the twin children in Rebecca's womb:

> *Being not yet born, neither having done any good or evil, that the purpose of God according to election might stand, not of works, but of him that calleth; it was said unto her, The elder shall serve the younger.*[217]

Accordingly, he refers to another prophetic witness, where it is written, "*Jacob have I loved, but Esau have I hated.*"[218] Then, realizing how what he said could disturb those whose understanding could not penetrate to this depth of grace, he adds: "*What shall we say then? Is there*

216. Romans 9:18.
217. Verses 11–12.
218. Verse 13; see Malachi 1:2–3.

unrighteousness with God? God forbid."[219] Yet it does seem unfair that, without any merit derived from good works or bad, God should love the one and hate the other. Now, if the apostle had wished us to understand that there were future good deeds of the one, and evil deeds of the other—which God, of course, foreknew—he would never have said "not of good works" but rather "of future works." Thus he would have solved the difficulty; or, rather, he would have left no difficulty to be solved. As it is, however, when he went on to exclaim, "God forbid!"—that is, "God forbid that there should be unfairness in God"—he proceeds immediately to add (to prove that no unfairness in God is involved here), *"For he saith to Moses, I will have mercy on whom I will have mercy, and I will have compassion on whom I will have compassion."*[220] Now, who but a fool would think God unfair either when He imposes penal judgment on the deserving or when He shows mercy to the undeserving? Finally, the apostle concludes and says, *"So then it is not of him that willeth, nor of him that runneth, but of God that sheweth mercy."*[221]

Thus, both the twins were *"by nature the children of wrath,"*[222] not because of any works of their own, but because they were both bound in the fetters of damnation originally forged by Adam. But He who said, *"I will have mercy on whom I will have mercy,"* loved Jacob in

219. Verse 14.
220. Verse 15.
221. Verse 16.
222. Ephesians 2:3.

unmerited mercy, yet hated Esau with merited justice. Since this judgment (of wrath) was due them both, the former learned from what happened to the other that the fact that he had not, with equal merit, incurred the same penalty gave him no ground to boast of his own distinctive merits—but, instead, that he should glory in the abundance of divine grace, because "*it is not of him who that willeth, nor of him that runneth, but of God that sheweth mercy.*" And, indeed, the whole visage of Scripture and, if I may speak so, the lineaments of its countenance, are found to exhibit a mystery, most profound and salutary, to admonish all who carefully look thereupon, "*He that glorieth, let him glory in the Lord.*"[223]

99. Now, after the apostle had commended God's mercy in saying, "*So then, it is not of him that willeth, nor of him that runneth, but of God that sheweth mercy,*" next in order he intends to speak also of His judgment—for where His mercy is not shown, it is not unfairness but justice. For with God there is no injustice. Thus, he immediately added, "*For the scripture saith unto Pharaoh, Even for this same purpose have I raised thee up, that I might shew my power in thee, and that my name might be declared throughout all the earth.*"[224] Then, having said this, he draws a conclusion that looks both ways, that is, toward mercy and

223. 1 Corinthians 1:31; see also Jeremiah 9:24. The religious intention of Augustine's emphasis upon divine sovereignty and predestination is never so much to account for the doom of the wicked as to underscore the sheer and wonderful gratuity of salvation.
224. Romans 9:17.

toward judgment: *"Therefore,"* he says, *"hath he mercy on whom he will have mercy, and whom he will he hardeneth."* He shows mercy out of His great goodness; He hardens out of no unfairness at all. In this way, neither does he who is saved have a basis for glorying in any merit of his own; nor does the man who is damned have a basis for complaining of anything except what he has fully merited. For grace alone separates the redeemed from the lost, all having been mingled together in the one mass of perdition, arising from a common cause which leads back to their common origin. But if any man hears this in such a way as to say: *"Why doth he yet find fault? For who hath resisted his will?"*[225]—as if to make it seem that man should not therefore be blamed for being evil because God *"hath mercy on whom he will have mercy, and whom he will he hardeneth"*—God forbid that we should be ashamed to give the same reply as we see the apostle giving: *"O man, who are thou that repliest against God? Shall the thing formed say to him that formed it, Why hast thou made me thus? Hath not the potter power over the clay, of the same lump to make one vessel unto honor, and another unto dishonor?"*[226]

There are some stupid men who think that in this part of the argument the apostle had no answer to give; and, for lack of a reasonable rejoinder, simply rebuked the audacity of his gainsayer. But what he said—*"O man, who are thou?"*—has actually great weight and in an argument like

225. Verse 19.
226. Verses 20–21.

this recalls man, in a single word, to consider the limits of his capacity and, at the same time, supplies an important explanation.

For if one does not understand these matters, who is he to talk back to God? And if one does understand, he finds no better ground even then for talking back. For if he understands, he sees that the whole human race was condemned in its apostate head by a divine judgment so just that not even if a single member of the race were ever saved from it, no one could rail against God's justice. And he also sees that those who are saved had to be saved on such terms that it would show—by contrast with the greater number of those not saved but simply abandoned to their wholly just damnation—what the whole mass deserved and to what end God's merited judgment would have brought them, had not His undeserved mercy interposed. Thus every mouth of those disposed to glory in their own merits should be stopped, so that *"he that glorieth, let him glory in the Lord."*

26

The Triumph of God's Sovereign Good Will

100. These are "the great works of the LORD, well-considered in all his acts of will"[227]—and so wisely well-considered that when His angelic and human creation sinned (that is, did not do what He willed, but what it willed) He could still accomplish what He Himself had willed and this through the same creaturely will by which the first act contrary to the Creator's will had been done. As the Supreme Good, He made good use of evil deeds, for the damnation of those whom He had justly predestined to punishment and for the salvation of those whom He had mercifully predestined to grace.

For, as far as they were concerned, they did what God did not will that they do, but as far as God's omnipotence is concerned, they were quite unable to achieve their purpose. In their very act of going against His will, His will was thereby accomplished. This is the meaning of the statement, "The works of the LORD are great, well-considered in all his acts of will"—that in a strange and ineffable fashion even that which is done against His will is not done without His will. For it would not be done without

227. Psalm 110:2 (Vulgate).

His allowing it—and surely His permission is not unwilling but willing—nor would He who is good allow the evil to be done, unless in His omnipotence He could bring good even out of evil.

101. Sometimes, however, a man of good will wills something that God doth not will, even though God's will is much more, and much more certainly, good—for under no circumstances can it ever be evil. For example, it is a good son's will that his father live, whereas it is God's good will that he should die. Or, again, it can happen that a man of evil will can will something that God also wills with a good will—as, for example, a bad son wills that his father die and this is also God's will. Of course, the former wills what God does not will, whereas the latter does will what God wills. Yet the piety of the one, though he wills not what God wills, is more consonant with God's will than is the impiety of the other, who wills the same thing that God wills. There is a very great difference between what is fitting for man to will and what is fitting for God—and also between the ends to which a man directs his will—and this difference determines whether an act of will is to be approved or disapproved. Actually, God achieves some of his purposes—which are, of course, all good—through the evil wills of bad men. For example, it was through the ill will of the Jews that, by the good will of the Father, Christ was slain for us—a deed so good that when the apostle Peter would have

nullified it he was called "Satan" by him who had come in order to be slain.[228]

How good seemed the purposes of the pious faithful who were unwilling that the apostle Paul should go to Jerusalem, lest there he should suffer the things that the prophet Agabus had predicted![229] And yet God had willed that he should suffer these things for the sake of the preaching of Christ, and for the training of a martyr for Christ. And this good purpose of His he achieved, not through the good will of the Christians, but through the ill will of the Jews. Yet they were more fully His who did not will what He willed than were those who were willing instruments of His purpose—for while he and the latter did the very same thing, He worked through them with a good will, whereas they did His good will with their ill will.

102. But, however strong the wills either of angels or of men, whether good or evil, whether they will what God wills or will something else, the will of the Omnipotent is always undefeated. And this will can never be evil, because even when it inflicts evils, it is still just; and obviously what is just is not evil. Therefore, whether through pity *"he hath mercy on whom he willeth,"* or in justice *"whom he will, he hardeneth,"* the omnipotent God never does anything except what He wills, and does everything that He wills.

228. See Matthew 16:23.
229. See Acts 21:10–12.

27

Limits of God's Plan for Human Salvation

103. Accordingly, when we hear and read in sacred Scripture that God *"will have all men to be saved,"*[230] although we know well enough that not all men are saved, we are not on that account to underrate the fully omnipotent will of God. Rather, we must understand the Scripture, *"Who will have all men to be saved,"* as meaning that no man is saved unless God wills his salvation: not that there is no man whose salvation He does not will, but that no one is saved unless He wills it. Moreover, His will should be sought in prayer, because if He wills, then what He wills must necessarily be. And, indeed, it was of prayer to God that the apostle was speaking when he made that statement. Thus, we are also to understand what is written in the gospel about Him *"which lighteth every man."*[231] This means that there is no man who is enlightened except by God.

In any case, the word concerning God, *"who will have all men to be saved,"* does not mean that there is no one whose salvation He does not will—He who was unwilling to work miracles among those who, He said, would have repented if He had wrought them—but by "all men" we are

230. 1 Timothy 2:4.
231. John 1:9.

to understand the whole of mankind, in every single group into which it can be divided: kings and subjects; nobility and plebeians; the high and the low; the learned and unlearned; the healthy and the sick; the bright, the dull, and the stupid; the rich, the poor, and the middle class; males, females, infants, children, the adolescent, young adults and middle-aged and very old; of every tongue and fashion, of all the arts, of all professions, with the countless variety of wills and minds and all the other things that differentiate people. For from which of these groups does not God will that some men from every nation should be saved through His only begotten Son our Lord? Therefore, He does save them since the Omnipotent cannot will in vain, whatsoever He wills.

Now, the apostle had enjoined that prayers should be offered "*for all men*"[232] and especially "*for kings, and for all that are in authority,*"[233] whose worldly pomp and pride could be supposed to be a sufficient cause for them to despise the humility of the Christian faith. Then, continuing his argument, "*for this is good and acceptable in the sight of God our Saviour*"[234]—that is, to pray even for such as these (kings)—the apostle, to remove any warrant for despair, added, "*Who will have all men to be saved, and come unto the knowledge of the truth.*"[235] Truly, then, God has judged it good that through the prayers of the

232. 1 Timothy 2:1.
233. Verse 2.
234. Verse 3.
235. Verse 4.

lowly He would deign to grant salvation to the exalted—a paradox we have already seen exemplified. Our Lord also uses the same manner of speech in the gospel, where he says to the Pharisees, *"Ye tithe mint and rue and all manner of herbs."*[236] Obviously, the Pharisees did not tithe what belonged to others, nor all the herbs of all the people of other lands. Therefore, just as we should interpret "every herb" to mean "every kind of herb," so also we can interpret "all men" to mean "all kinds of men." We could interpret it in any other fashion, as long as we are not compelled to believe that the Omnipotent hath willed anything to be done which was not done. *"Whatsoever the LORD pleased, that did he in heaven, and in earth, in the seas, and all deep places,"*[237] as truth sings of Him, and surely He has not willed to do anything that He has not done. There must be no equivocation on this point.

236. Luke 11:42.
237. Psalm 135:6.

28

The Destiny of Man

104. Consequently, God would have willed to preserve even the first man in that state of salvation in which he was created and would have brought him in due season, after the begetting of children, to a better state without the intervention of death—where he not only would have been unable to sin, but would not have had even the will to sin—if He had foreknown that man would have had a steadfast will to continue without sin, as he had been created to do. But since He did foreknow that man would make bad use of his free will—that is, that he would sin—God prearranged His own purpose so that He could do good to man, even in man's doing evil, and so that the good will of the Omnipotent should be nullified by the bad will of men, but should nonetheless be fulfilled.

105. Thus it was fitting that man should be created, in the first place, so that he could will both good and evil—not without reward, if he willed the good; not without punishment, if he willed the evil. But in the future life he will not have the power to will evil; and yet this will not thereby restrict his free will. Indeed, his will will be much freer, because he will then have no power whatever to serve sin. For we surely ought not to find fault with such

a will, nor say it is no will, or that it is not rightly called free, when we so desire happiness that we not only are unwilling to be miserable, but have no power whatsoever to will it.

And, just as in our present state, our soul is unable to will unhappiness for ourselves, so then it will be forever unable to will iniquity. But the ordered course of God's plan was not to be passed by, wherein He willed to show how good the rational creature is that is able not to sin, although one unable to sin is better.[238] So, too, it was an inferior order of immortality—but yet it was immortality—in which man was capable of not dying, even if the higher order which is to be is one in which man will be incapable of dying.[239]

106. Human nature lost the former kind of immortality through the misuse of free will. It is to receive the latter through grace—though it was to have obtained it through merit, if it had not sinned. Not even then, however, could there have been any merit without grace. For although sin had its origin in free will alone, still free will would not have been sufficient to maintain justice, save as divine aid had been afforded man, in the gift of participation in

---

238. Another example of Augustine's wordplay. Man's original capacities included both the power not to sin and the power to sin (*posse non peccare et posse peccare*). In Adam's original sin, man lost the *posse non peccare* (the power not to sin) and retained the posse peccare (the power to sin)—which he continues to exercise. In the fulfillment of grace, man will have the *posse peccare* taken away and receive the highest of all, the power not to be able to sin, *non posse peccare*. See also *On Correction and Grace*, Ch. 33.

239. Again, a wordplay between *posset non mori* and *non possit mori*.

the immutable good. Thus, for example, the power to die when he wills it is in a man's own hands—since there is no one who could not kill himself by not eating (not to mention other means). But the bare will is not sufficient for maintaining life, if the aids of food and other means of preservation are lacking.

Similarly, man in paradise was capable of self-destruction by abandoning justice by an act of will; yet if the life of justice was to be maintained, his will alone would not have sufficed, unless He who made him had given him aid. But, after the fall, God's mercy was even more abundant, for then the will itself had to be freed from the bondage in which sin and death are the masters. There is no way at all by which it can be freed by itself, but only through God's grace, which is made effectual in the faith of Christ. Thus, as it is written, even the will by which "the will itself is prepared by the Lord"[240] so that we may receive the other gifts of God through which we come to the Gift eternal—this too comes from God.

107. Accordingly, even the life eternal, which is surely the wages of good works, is called a gift of God by the apostle. *"For the wages of sin,"* he says, *"is death; but the gift of God is eternal life through Christ Jesus our Lord."*[241] Now, wages for military service are paid as a just debit, not as a gift. Hence, he said *"the wages of sin is death,"* to show that death was not an unmerited punishment for sin but

240. See Proverbs 8:35 (Septuagint).

241. Romans 6:23.

a just debit. But a gift, unless it be gratuitous, is not grace. We are, therefore, to understand that even man's merited goods are gifts from God, and when life eternal is given through them, what else do we have but "grace upon grace returned"[242]?

Man was, therefore, made upright, and in such a fashion that he could either continue in that uprightness—though not without divine aid—or become perverted by his own choice. Whichever of these two man had chosen, God's will would be done, either by man or at least concerning him. Wherefore, since man chose to do his own will instead of God's, God's will concerning him was done; for, from the same mass of perdition that flowed out of that common source, God makes *"one vessel unto honour, and another unto dishonour"*[243]; the ones for honorable use through His mercy, the ones for ignoble use through His judgment; lest anyone glory in man, or—what is the same thing—in himself.

108. Now, we could not be redeemed, even through *"one mediator between God and men, the man Christ Jesus,"*[244] if he were not also God. For when Adam was made—being made an upright man—there was no need for a mediator. Once sin, however, had widely separated the human race from God, it was necessary for a mediator, who alone was born, lived, and was put to death without

242. See John 1:16.
243. Romans 9:21.
244. 1 Timothy 2:5.

sin, to reconcile us to God, and provide even for our bodies a resurrection to life eternal—and all this in order that man's pride might be exposed and healed through God's humility. Thus it might be shown man how far he had departed from God, when by the incarnate God he is recalled to God; that man in his contumacy might be furnished an example of obedience by the God-Man; that the fount of grace might be opened up; that even the resurrection of the body—itself promised to the redeemed—might be previewed in the resurrection of the Redeemer Himself; that the devil might be vanquished by that very nature he was rejoicing over having deceived—all this, however, without giving man ground for glory in himself, lest pride spring up anew. And if there are other advantages accruing from so great a mystery of the Mediator, which those who profit from them can see or testify—even if they cannot be described—let them be added to this list.

29

"The Last Things"

109. Now, for the time that intervenes between man's death and the final resurrection, there is a secret shelter for his soul, as each is worthy of rest or affliction according to what it has merited while it lived in the body.

110. There is no denying that the souls of the dead are benefited by the piety of their living friends, when the sacrifice of the Mediator is offered for the dead, or alms are given in the church. But these means benefit only those who, when they were living, have merited that such services could be of help to them. For there is a mode of life that is neither so good as not to need such helps after death nor so bad as not to gain benefit from them after death. There is, however, a good mode of life that does not need such helps, and, again, one so thoroughly bad that, when such a man departs this life, such helps avail him nothing. It is here, then, in this life, that all merit or demerit is acquired whereby a man's condition in the life hereafter is improved or worsened. Therefore, let no one hope to obtain any merit with God after he is dead that he has neglected to obtain here in this life.

So, then, those means that the church constantly uses in interceding for the dead are not opposed to that statement of the apostle when he said, "*For we must all appear before the judgment seat of Christ; that every one may receive the things done in his body, according to that he hath done, whether it be good or bad.*"[245] For each man has for himself while living in the body earned the merit whereby these means can benefit him (after death), for they do not benefit all. And yet why should they not benefit all, unless it be because of the different kinds of lives men lead in the body? Accordingly, when sacrifices, whether of the altar or of alms, are offered for the baptized dead, they are thank offerings for the very good, propitiations for the not-so-very-bad (*non valde malis*), and, as for the very bad—even if they are of no help to the dead—they are at least a sort of consolation to the living. Where they are of value, their benefit consists either in obtaining a full forgiveness or, at least, in making damnation more tolerable.

111. After the resurrection, however, when the general judgment has been held and finished, the boundary lines will be set for the two cities: the one of Christ, the other of the devil; one for the good, the other for the bad—both including angels and men. In the one group, there will be no will to sin, in the other, no power to sin, nor any further possibility of dying. The citizens of the first commonwealth will go on living truly and happily in life eternal. The second will go on, miserable in death eternal, with no power to die to it. The condition of both societies will

245. 2 Corinthians 5:10.

then be fixed and endless. But in the first city, some will outrank others in bliss, and in the second, some will have a more tolerable burden of misery than others.

112. It is quite in vain, then, that some—indeed very many—yield to merely human feelings and deplore the notion of the eternal punishment of the damned and their interminable and perpetual misery. They do not believe that such things will be. Not that they would go counter to divine Scripture—but, yielding to their own human feelings, they soften what seems harsh and give a milder emphasis to statements they believe are meant more to terrify than to express the literal truth. "God will not forget," they say, "to show mercy, nor in His anger will He shut up His mercy." This is, in fact, the text of a holy psalm.[246] But there is no doubt that it is to be interpreted to refer to those who are called *"vessels of mercy,"*[247] those who are freed from misery not by their own merits but through God's mercy. Even so, if they suppose that the text applies to all men, there is no ground for them further to suppose that there can be an end for those of whom it is said, *"And these shall go away into everlasting punishment."*[248] Otherwise, it can as well be thought that there will also be an end to the happiness of those of whom the antithesis was said: "But the righteous into life eternal."

246. See Psalm 77:9.
247. Romans 9:23.
248. Matthew 25:46.

But let them suppose, if it pleases them, that, for certain intervals of time, the punishments of the damned are somewhat mitigated. Even so, the wrath of God must be understood as still resting on them. And this is damnation—for this anger, which is not a violent passion in the divine mind, is called "wrath" in God. Yet even in His wrath—His wrath resting on them—He does not "shut up His mercy." This is not to put an end to their eternal afflictions, but rather to apply or interpose some little respite in their torments. For the psalm does not say, "To put an end to His wrath," or, "After His wrath," but, "*In His wrath.*" Now, if this wrath were all there is (in man's damnation), and even if it were present only in the slightest degree conceivable—still, to be lost out of the kingdom of God, to be an exile from the City of God, to be estranged from the life of God, to suffer loss of the great abundance of God's blessings that He has hidden for those who fear Him and prepared for those who hope in Him[249]—this would be a punishment so great that, if it be eternal, no torments that we know could be compared to it, no matter how many ages they continued.

113. The eternal death of the damned—that is, their estrangement from the life of God—will therefore abide without end, and it will be common to them all, no matter what some people, moved by their human feelings, may wish to think about gradations of punishment, or the

249. See Psalm 31:19.

relief or intermission of their misery. In the same way, the eternal life of the saints will abide forever, and also be common to all of them no matter how different the grades of rank and honor in which they shine forth in their effulgent harmony.

The Principles of Christian Living: Faith and Hope

114. Thus, from our confession of faith, briefly summarized in the Creed (which is milk for babes when pondered at the carnal level but food for strong men when it is considered and studied spiritually), there is born the good hope of the faithful, accompanied by a holy love.[250] But of these affirmations, all of which ought faithfully to be believed, only those which have to do with hope are contained in the Lord's Prayer. For "cursed be the man," as the divine eloquence testified, *"that trusteth in man."*[251] Thus, he who rests his hope in himself is bound by the bond of this curse. Therefore, we should seek from none other than the Lord God whatever it is that we hope to do well, or hope to obtain as reward for our good works.

115. Accordingly, in the evangelist Matthew, the Lord's Prayer may be seen to contain seven petitions: three of them ask for eternal goods, the other four for temporal goods, which are, however, necessary for obtaining the eternal goods.

250. Note the artificial return to the triadic scheme of the treatise: faith, hope, and love.

251. Jeremiah 17:5.

For when we say: *"Hallowed be thy name. Thy kingdom come, Thy will be done in earth, as it is in heaven"*[252]this last being wrongly interpreted by some as meaning "in body and spirit"—these blessings will be retained forever. They begin in this life, of course; they are increased in us as we make progress, but in their perfection—which is to be hoped for in the other life—they will be possessed forever! But when we say: *"Give us this day our daily bread. And forgive us our debts, as we forgive our debtors. And lead us not into temptation, but deliver us from evil,"*[253] who does not see that all these pertain to our needs in the present life? In that life eternal—where we all hope to be—the hallowing of God's name, His kingdom, and His will, in our spirit and body will abide perfectly and immortally. But in this life we ask for *"daily bread"* because it is necessary, in the measure required by soul and body, whether we take the term in a spiritual or bodily sense, or both. And here too it is that we petition for forgiveness, where the sins are committed; here too are the temptations that allure and drive us to sinning; here, finally, the evil from which we wish to be freed. But in that other world none of these things will be found.

116. However, the evangelist Luke, in his version of the Lord's Prayer, has brought together, not seven, but five petitions. Yet, obviously, there is no discrepancy here, but rather, in his brief way, the evangelist has shown us how

252. Matthew 6:9–10.
253. Verses 11–13.

the seven petitions should be understood. Actually, God's name is even now hallowed in the spirit, but the kingdom of God is yet to come in the resurrection of the body. Therefore, Luke was seeking to show that the third petition ("*Thy will be done*") is a repetition of the first two, and makes this better understood by omitting it. He then adds three other petitions, concerning daily bread, forgiveness of sins, and avoidance of temptation.[254] However, what Matthew puts in the last place, *"But deliver us from evil,"* Luke leaves out, in order that we might understand that it was included in what was previously said about temptation. This is, indeed, why Matthew said, *"But deliver us,"* instead of, "And deliver us," as if to indicate that there is only one petition—"Will not this, but that"—so that anyone would realize that he is being delivered from evil in that he is not being led into temptation.

254. See Luke 11:2–4.

31

Love

117. And now regarding love, which the apostle says is greater than the other two—that is, faith and hope—for the more richly it dwells in a man, the better the man in whom it dwells. For when we ask whether someone is a good man, we are not asking what he believes, or hopes, but what he loves. Now, beyond all doubt, he who loves aright believes and hopes rightly. Likewise, he who does not love believes in vain, even if what he believes is true; he hopes in vain, even if what he hopes for is generally agreed to pertain to true happiness, unless he believes and hopes for this: that he may through prayer obtain the gift of love. For, although it is true that he cannot hope without love, it may be that there is something without which, if he does not love it, he cannot realize the object of his hopes. An example of this would be if a man hopes for life eternal—and who is there who does not love that?—and yet does not love righteousness, without which no one comes to it.

Now this is the true faith of Christ which the apostle commends: faith that works through love. And what it yet lacks in love it asks that it may receive, it seeks that it may find, and knocks that it may be opened unto it.[255] For faith achieves what the law commands (*fides namque impetrat quod lex imperat*). And, without the gift of God—that is, without the Holy Spirit, through whom love is shed abroad in our hearts—the law may bid but it cannot aid (*jubere lex poterit, non juvare*). Moreover, it can make of man a transgressor, who cannot then excuse himself by pleading ignorance. For appetite reigns where the love of God does not.[256]

118. When, in the deepest shadows of ignorance, he lives according to the flesh with no restraint of reason—this is the primal state of man.[257] Afterward, when "*for by the law is the knowledge of sin*"[258] has come to man, and the Holy Spirit has not yet come to his aid—so that even if he wishes to live according to the law, he is vanquished—man sins knowingly and is brought under the spell and made the slave of sin, "*for of whom a man is overcome, of the same is he brought in bondage*"[259]. The effect of the knowledge of the law is that sin works in man the whole round of concupiscence, which adds to the guilt of the first transgression. And thus it is that what was written is fulfilled: "*The law entered, that*

---

255. See Matthew 7:7.
256. Another wordplay on *cupiditas* and *caritas*.
257. An interesting resemblance here to Freud's description of the Id, the primal core of our unconscious life.
258. Romans 3:20.
259. 2 Peter 2:19.

the offense might abound."[260] This is the second state of man.[261]

But if God regards a man with solicitude so that he then believes in God's help in fulfilling His commands, and if a man begins to be led by the Spirit of God, then the mightier power of love struggles against the power of the flesh.[262] And although there is still in man a power that fights against him—his infirmity being not yet fully healed—yet he (the righteous man) lives by faith and lives righteously in so far as he does not yield to evil desires, conquering them by his love of righteousness. This is the third stage of the man of good hope.

A final peace is in store for him who continues to go forward in this course toward perfection through steadfast piety. This will be perfected beyond this life in the repose of the spirit, and, at the last, in the resurrection of the body.

Of these four different stages of man, the first is before the law, the second is under the law, the third is under grace, and the fourth is in full and perfect peace. Thus, also, the history of God's people has been ordered by successive temporal epochs, as it pleased God, who "ordered all things in measure and number and weight."[263] The first period was before the law; the

260. Romans 5:20.

261. Compare the psychological notion of the effect of external moral pressures and their power to arouse guilt feelings, as in Freud's notion of "superego."

262. See Galatians 5:17.

263. Wisdom of Solomon 11:20 (Apocrypha).

second under the law, which was given through Moses; the next, under grace that was revealed through the first advent of the Mediator.[264] This grace was not previously absent from those to whom it was to be imparted, although, in conformity to the temporal dispensations, it was veiled and hidden. For none of the righteous men of antiquity could find salvation apart from the faith of Christ. And, unless Christ had also been known to them, He could not have been prophesied to us—sometimes openly and sometimes obscurely—through their ministry.

119. Now, in whichever of these four "ages"—if one can call them that—the grace of regeneration finds a man, then and there all his past sins are forgiven him and the guilt he contracted in being born is removed by his being reborn. And so true is it that *"the wind bloweth where it listeth"*[265] that some men have never known the second "age" of slavery under the law, but begin to have divine aid directly under the new commandment.

120. Yet, before a man can receive the commandment, he must, of course, live according to the flesh. But, once he has been imbued with the sacrament of rebirth, no harm will come to him even if he then immediately depart this life—*"For to this end Christ both died, and rose, and revived, that he might be Lord both of the dead and living."*[266] Nor will

264. See John 1:17.
265. John 3:8.
266. Romans 14:9.

the kingdom of death have dominion over him for whom He, who was "free among the dead,"[267] died.

267. See Psalm 88:5.

32

The End of All the Law

121. All the divine precepts are, therefore, referred back to love, of which the apostle says, "*Now the end of the commandment is* [love] *out of a pure heart, and a good conscience, and of faith unfeigned.*"[268] Thus every commandment harks back to love. For whatever one does either in fear of punishment or from some carnal impulse, so that it does not measure up to the standard of love that the Holy Spirit sheds abroad in our hearts—whatever it is, it is not yet done as it should be, although it may seem to be. Love, in this context, of course includes both the love of God and the love of our neighbor and, indeed, "*on these two commandments hang all the law and the prophets*"[269]—and, we may add, the gospel and the apostles, for from nowhere else comes the voice, "*The end of the commandment is* [love]," and, "*God is love.*"[270]

Therefore, whatsoever things God commands (and one of these is, "*Thou shalt not commit adultery*"[271]) and whatsoever things are not positively ordered but are strongly advised as good spiritual counsel (and one of

268. 1 Timothy 1:5.
269. Matthew 22:40.
270. 1 John 4:16.
271. Exodus 20:14.

these is, *"It is good for a man not to touch a woman"*[272])—all of these imperatives are rightly obeyed only when they are measured by the standard of our love of God and our love of our neighbor in God (*propter Deum*). This applies both in the present age and in the world to come. Now we love God in faith; then, at sight.

For, though mortal men ourselves, we do not know the hearts of mortal men. But then *"the Lord…will bring to light the hidden things of darkness, and will make manifest the counsels of the hearts: and then shall every man have praise of God"*[273]for what will be praised and loved in a neighbor by his neighbor is just that which, lest it remain hidden, God Himself will bring to light. Moreover, passion decreases as love increases[274] until love comes at last to that fullness that cannot be surpassed, *"greater love hath no man than this, that a man lay down his life for his friends."*[275] Who, then, can explain how great the power of love will be, when there will be no passion (*cupiditas*) for it to restrain or overcome? For, then, the supreme state of true health (*summa sanitas*) will have been reached, when the struggle with death shall be no more.

---

272. 1 Corinthians 7:1.
273. 1 Corinthians 4:5.
274. *Minuitur autem cupiditas caritate crescente.*
275. John 15:13.

33

Conclusion

122. But somewhere this book must have an end. You can see for yourself whether you should call it an Enchiridion, or use it as one. But since I have judged that your zeal in Christ ought not to be spurned and since I believe and hope for good things for you through the help of our Redeemer, and since I love you greatly as one of the members of His body, I have written this book for you—may its usefulness match its prolixity!—on Faith, Hope, and Love.